THE
FASHION

VOLUME III

Cover Credits:
Photo by: Peter Brown assisted by Lester
Model: Astrid at Premier
Make up: Debbie Bunn
Hair: James Lebon/Cuts Co.
Styled by: Iain R. Webb
Designed by: The Fish Family

First published in Great Britain in 1985 by Zomba Books,
Zomba House, 165-167 Willesden High Road,
London NW10 2SG

© Zomba Books

ISBN 0 946391 67 X

Typeset by Capital Setters

Printed by Baker Bros Ltd. Pontefract, West Yorkshire.

Designed by The Fish Family

Edited by Iain R. Webb/Lorraine Johnston

Production Services by Book Production Consultants, Cambridge

First Edition

THE FASHION YEAR

EDITED BY Lorraine Johnston

CONSULTANT EDITOR Iain R. Webb

VOLUME III

ZOMBA BOOKS

Thanks to
Louise Gillic
Ben
Nick Knight
Mark Goddard
Neil Dell
Our Parents

Dedicated to Jake Wynter

CONTENTS

YOU EITHER HAVE OR YOU HAVEN'T GOT...

'Fashion is one helluva curious business,' said Alice, as the White Rabbit pulled the large gold fob watch from his pocket and anchored it firmly to his lapel . . . '
Like make-believe, Fashion can make a fool of you.

What most don't realise is that clothes are capable of revealing more than they cover. Neatly finished seams do nothing to conceal the gaping holes in one's own psyche. You expect too much if you imagine that by donning a certain length of skirt, or wildly patterned shirt it will make you belong. Invariably it will only distract the eye for a moment. How long will it be before someone realises that the purpose of gaudy wrapping paper is to enhance the present within . . . not make up for it.

Over the year we have seen some real *gaudy wrapping* paraded before us. More than usual, in fact, for it was during this particular year that Fashion decided to go overground.

How many times was the line, 'Not since the '60s . . . ' used when referring to the boom being experienced by the Fashion industry? Quite simply, because, *not since the '60s* has this commodity 'Fashion' been so widely desired, or worn in various guises by so many.

There are no longer just a few eccentrically dressed young things calling themselves, 'Individuals'. Now everyone wants to be IN, and every High Street chainstore has realised the potential of the pose, utilising elaborate 'fashion extravaganzas', and mobilizing expertly trained teams of stylish troubleshooters to create brilliantly photographed pseudo-trendsetting campaigns. Models strike poses on the pages of magazines which are then copied ad infinitum by ad agencies, and a new 'elite' of young pretenders are happy to be wrapping themselves in this season's accepted form of elitism, be it patent shoes; diamanté brooches; polo necks; or wearing your shirt tails flapping outside your pants. 'Style' has gone mainstream. A whole new generation of children are being born with Designer Genes. It has reached the masses, it is also outmoded and for that reason is no longer desirable to The Few.

Not so long ago people would have died for *style* (some did – witness Edie Sedgewick). To be told you had style was the greatest of accolades, yet here we are in 1985 with everything turned back to front, and upside down along with the clothes.

Earlier in the year the *Face* magazine (viewed the world over as *the* Bible of Style) printed a paragraph which supported its decision to replace 'Style' with 'Fashion' within its pages, because the former had 'assumed such poncey and pretentious connotations'.

Isn't this where we came in?

Today Style has become merely styling. Anyone can have it. Most have gleaned it from magazines, of favourite pop personalities who present over-proportioned images which can easily be remade to fit any size, or shape. How unstylish!

There are still, however, a certain amount of people who most definitely have something of their own. I can think of a handful of creative people whom I may meet at any time on *any* occasion who will always be dressed just so . . . or so: make-up artist – Yvonne Gold, hairdresser – James Lebon, BodyMap's textile designer – Hilde Smith, stylist – Ray Petri, Tina Chow, designer – Riffat Ozbeck. These people all have what I term 'suss'. Their dressing is intuitive, their lifestyles reflective.

Several years ago Rae Spencer Cullin (Miss Mouse) laid down a series of rules for the culturally aware cognescenti she called the Fashion Police. These officers of Style were to aid the public into a state of artistic well being.

Now that the streets have become a tougher place to be, and policing has taken turn to the right new laws are indeed necessary.

● The White Rabbit courtesy of Thomas Nelson Publisher, from *The Magic of Lewis Carroll*

THE SUSS LAWS

1   Never be afraid to admit to stealing from anyone – but justify these actions by deeming yourself *eclectic* as opposed to a petty criminal.

2   Always think before you dress. For consider that when arresting attention anything you say (in the way in which you dress) could be taken down and one day used in evidence against you.

3   Never make any (definitive) statements which cannot be retracted, or at the very least modified at a later date. For, this week's highbrow will undoubtedly become next week's High Street.

4   If you choose to clothe yourself in the dress of the criminal fraternity (not to be confused with the Preppy ideal) you must be prepared to spend a certain amount of your time in solitary.

5   In order to keep an easy mind, realise that miscarriages of justice are inevitable. An illusion which has taken you hours to create – that wondrous palor you desire – may look to others like a severe case of life imprisonment. 'How often do they let you out of your cell?', they ask concernedly.

6   Each article of clothing you wear can say something by itself, but remember that it is not always necessary to string them together logically when making a statement. Simple words may be shorter than sentences, but they will often say more about you than a whole paragraph ever can.

7   When striving to follow Fashion Editors never ending advice on how to update your wardrobe to that particular season, do not be fooled into believing that by simply adding the very latest trendy *de rigeur* item to your wardrobe you will create the total look you are searching for. These people are merely accessories to the crime. ie. Sticking a picture on your back does not make you a BUFFALO – more likely a *bewildered beast!*

8   A Victim of Fashion is not someone who can be held responsible for their misfortune. In much the same way that nobody ever asks to be mugged – clothes do have a way of overpowering the innocent and leaving them for dead.

9   Coveting the very latest Fashions because you believe them to be just that is not a crime . . . until you are apprehended leaving the store with them.

10   (Social) Suicide is no longer a punishable crime offence. However, it is not a solution, but merely an effect of your dress sense. There are desirable alternatives. (See the careers of Andrew Logan; Anna Piaggi.)

11   A clever forgery can only receive the attention it deserves when viewed alongside the original!

For future reference: People who possess 'suss' are never to be seen on the wrong side of the Law, because they are laws unto themselves. They are invariably to be found holding up bars rather than behind them.

THE COLLECTIONS

LONDON, PARIS, MILAN, NEW YORK AND TOKYO

LONDON

JASPER CONRAN ● Must be utterly sick of people calling him 'poor little rich boy' but the family coffers have enabled him to produce clothes in superb fabrics and maintain a high standard. Can that be bad? (S. Times)

JASPER CONRAN

JASPER CONRAN ● Great winter collection. (Honey)

KATHARINE HAMNETT

KATHARINE HAMNETT ● A designer for modern living, she

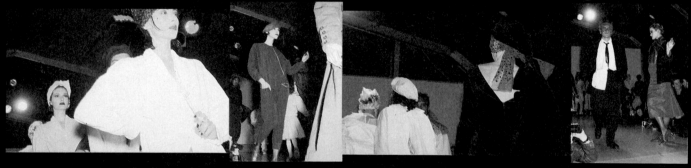

introduced us to the crumpled look and now seems to be

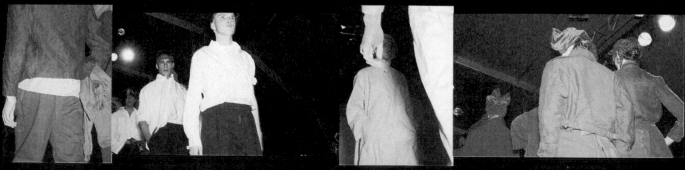

moving back to suits and sex for girls. (YOU)

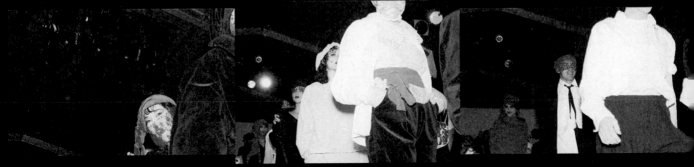

HYPER-HYPER ● **Is almost impossible to assess fairly.**

Like the curate's egg it's good in some parts and not so hot

in others. (S. Times)

HYPER HYPER ● Young, Bright, Exciting, it shouldn't try to be

anything different. (YOU)

BETTY JACKSON

BETTY JACKSON ● More commercial and less directional.

JOSEPH

The Americans loved it. (YOU)

JOHN ROCHA

ZANDRA RHODES

ZANDRA RHODES ● **One feels that her designs are more like**

works of art created to decorate walls than to wear. (S. Times)

BERNSTOCK & SPEIRS

de VRIES

ENGLISH ECCENTRICS

ENGLISH ECCENTRICS ● Pleasantly surprising. (YOU)

JOHN GALLIANO

JOHN GALLIANO ● British entertainment at its best. (Honey)

JOHN GALLIANO ● **He has a long way to go before I am**

absolutely convinced there isn't a touch of the Emperor's

New Clothes about some of his designs. (S. Times)

PARIS

DOROTHY BIS ● **The clothes have youthful, captivating appeal. Though French, the house has a certain clean American gusto.** (S. Times)

DOROTHY BIS

CASTLEBAJAC

COMME DES GARCONS

COMME DES GARCON ● Wonderful & innovative. (Honey)

KANSAI

THE FRENCH ● 'A woman is a woman and should show it

KOSHINO **LAGERFELD**

to the world', the androgynous look was not a hit. (YOU)

MONTANA

MONTANA ● This man grows in stature every season.(S. Times)

MUGLER

THIERRY MUGLER ● A travesty of how to steal from the past.
(YOU)

ARMANI

BYBLOS

COMPLICE

ERREUNO

FENDI

17

FERRE

SOPRANI

VERSACE

GIANNI VERSACE ● **A glamorous talent: he grows on you. His clothes are subtle and understated like his serpentine dresses. His appreciation of femininity is absolutely Italian and extremely sexy.** (S. Times)

NEW YORK

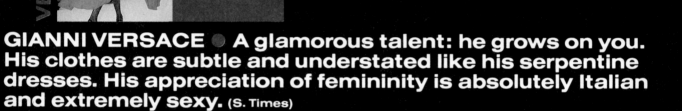

BEENE

BLASS

DE LA RENTA

NORMA KAMALI ● **Swimwear seems to be her best line.** (Honey)

ELLIS

KAMALI

LAUREN

A. KLEIN

TOKYO

THE JAPANESE SCHOOL ● **A very 'iffy' school indeed. Some of the clothes are admirable for their simplicity others are so**

ABE

HISHINUMA

IKEDA

KATO

complicated they would confuse even the most dedicated of

KIKUCHI

KOGA

KUMAGAI

SATO

their followers. However, I'm told by a few disciples that once

SHINZAKI

TAYAMA

a fan, they find it uncomfortable to wear anything else. (S. Times)

RACHEL AUBURN/LEIGH BOWERY ● Keeps the Americans happy. (Honey)

BODYMAP ● A commercial collection for the States this year, with some very desirable items. (YOU)

CHLOE ● When Karl Lagerfeld designed for the House its collections looked both sumptuous and pretty. Now they have three designers the clothes lack any personal conviction. (S. Times)

WENDY DAGWORTHY ● Has improved with age! – well designed format. (Honey)

JEAN PAUL GAULTIER ● The closest a frenchman has ever come to being English, he makes sex out of London's street savvy and is obsessed with cone-shaped bosoms but I forgive him that, definitely the name of the moment. (YOU)

BETTY JACKSON ● Her talent is unquestionable. I like some of her clothes more than others: I don't think her forte is grand occasion garments but her better clothes are absolutely original. (S. Times)

KENZO ● For old women. (Honey)

MONTANA ● Wonderfully theatrical, he's no longer a fashion leader but a great stylist. (YOU)

JEAN MUIR ● Is impeccable. Unquestionably a designer who combines great talent with integrity. She is one of the few British designers who is able to lure top French fashion editors over to see her shows. (S. Times)

HYPER-HYPER ● A great showcase for young talent. (Honey)

MISSONI ● I don't go to Italian shows, I find it too boring. (YOU)

COLLECTION QUOTES
PAT CROUCH ● Honey Magazine
LINDA McLEAN ● YOU Magazine
MERIEL McCOOEY ● The Sunday Times Magazine

COLLECTION PHOTOGRAPHERS
Gillian Campbell ● London and Paris
Niall McInerny ● Milan and New York
Wolfe Schuffner ● Tokyo

IN THE STYLE OF.....

The year through the eyes of London's premier style councillors

Boot face. Boot camp. The sleeping Bootie. In fashion there's nothing like a kick in the...

Autumn Boot: Manolo Blahnik
Riding Outfit: Hackett.

In fashion one has to get the bit between one's teeth. Fall '85 Mode: La Chasse.

Autumn Jewellery: Monty Don.
Riding Outfit: Hackett.

23

The pneumatic Amazons of comic strip lore range from supernatural sirens like Vampirella to the coyly criminal Cat-woman. Embodied by Jane Fonda in Vadim's *Barbarella*, and made art by Roy Lichtenstein in the sixties, the image and proportions of these superwomen continue to haunt the imagination, and have made themselves felt in the work of some of summer's most adventurous designers.

>100

Yellow plastic sequinned mini-dress, about £600; transparent yellow plastic mac, to order; both by Stephen Sprouse, at Browns, 23-27 South Molton St, W.1

< 212

a loyal workforce. They are the backbone of Hermès. Ironically, our current volume of sales is unprecedented: the obsession with mass-production has stabilised, traditional workmanship has been re-evaluated, and the public are appreciating the worth – and cost – of quality."

This confidence is reflected in the recent appointment of Eric Bergère, who is now designing Hermès ready-to-wear. "The marriage of tradition with fashion" is how his progressive employer describes his role at the house. Twenty-four years old, he graduated from the Paris fashion college of Esmod with first prize, and trained briefly with Mugler. He is aware of the challenge he took up when he chose to design a fresh image for the Hermès woman.

"They wanted me to achieve this without making a conspicuous statement: I set about reinvigorating the spirit of the collection with a mixture of discretion and humour. My objective: classic elegance." The results are sophisticated enough for

HERMES   HISTORY EMBELLISHED

established clients, yet possessed of a subversive dialect which appeals to Paris's most chic young street élite: the stage appears to be set for Hermès' youngest protegé to approach the limelight – in true house style.

CAROLINE KELLETT

Eric Bergère's sketch for his summer 1985 Business Suit, *main picture.*
Eric Bergère, *top right,* photographed on the shop's roof terrace, **Faubourg Saint Honoré.**
Insets: examples of Hermès' summer 1985 ready-to-wear collection

27

MICHAEL ROBERTS

Michael Roberts was once Fashion Editor of The SUNDAY TIMES newspaper. He then took the position of Style Editor at TATLER, and also Fashion Editor of VANITY magazine in the States. He is looked upon as one of the great style arbitors of our time. He is known for his cutting wit, and precise photographic pastiches.

●photographs by HERB RITTS

CAROLINE BAKER

Caroline Baker began as Fashion Editor of NOVA the highly visual sixties/early seventies magazine. She then became Fashion Editor of COSMOPOLITAN, and has since gone freelance which involves such names as I-D, The FACE, and numerous prestigious Italian fashion journals. She styles Katharine Hamnetts' catwalk shows, with the same spirited disregard for the clothes as she has throughout her career.

●photographs by NEIL KIRK & ROBERT ERDMAN

CAROLINE KELLETT

Began her first full-time job with VOGUE after leaving Oxford with a history degree, 3½ years ago. As both writer and stylist her initial province was the fashion features of the monthly Cue pages: subsequent to their consolidation she has worked on More Dash than Cash; compiles an anecdotal page, 'spy' in conjunction with the 'Cue' feature and covers and edits the International Ready To Wear collections, twice a year, in addition to her regular features.

AMANDA GRIEVE

Her career has included working as Junior Fashion Editor of HARPERS AND QUEEN magazine, and freelancing for numerous style journals including The FACE and I-D. She is now involved with the John Galliano organisation, styling his seasonal catwalk shows. Amanda is seen as being the prime protagonist of the 'shrubs as accessories' look which swept through fashion pictures this year.

●photographs by ANDREW MACPHERSON

RUNWAY REVOLUTION

Taking steps in the right direction

MIKEL ROSEN

I am given a collection of clothes – a stage and platform – a group of models – lights – some seats in some space – sound – a team of helpers. I am then expected to create an image/ atmosphere that will change the look of Fashion.

With the help of strong designers, you can almost do it – with the addition of hair-dressers, stylists, make-up artists, stage technicians and set design you have virtually done it. Finally, by adding the correct concept to each collection you have it!

Today, 1985, the majority of the competitive fashion world feel it necessary to launch their designs by presenting their collections in the form of a show on a catwalk, twice a year. March is the time to unveil the next Autumn/Winter collections and October is the month for viewing the Spring/ Summer wardrobe of the following year. This being the first time the fashion press and buyers see the new ranges of clothes, the pressure for the designers is intense – they have to convince the audience how strong the look is. For example, in March 1985, there were at least thirty-five designer shows. Four of those were group designer shows, two were college designer shows and six were new young designer shows exhibiting on a catwalk for the first time. The pressure on all concerned is immense. However, if the show production elements are in keeping

with the clothes the fashion message should not fail. For example, the younger international designers presenting their clothes with shock tactics or the established classic designers displaying their ranges with sophistication. In 1985 the high street retailer also has become a designer. At this level the mood is different again, the fashion show is used as a vehicle for press exposure to later gain the attention of the consumer.

I have chosen the following designers as examples of how different collections can be interpreted through various form of show presentation.

FASHION SCHOOLS

The colleges and polytechnics present the birth of new design ideas every summer – at B.A. or M.A. level where some of the most innovative and inspirational fashion ideas are created. The competition is intense, with forty to forty-five students graduating from St. Martins School of Art alone. It is not only a matter of gaining a B.A. degree but also a matter of surviving in the fashion business. These shows have become a regular event, and the feeling is one of a party. Models are allowed to parade on the catwalk doing their own thing and the atmosphere is one of fun. Who is the star going to be this

year? In the Summer of 1984 we had the success of John Galliano, who has gone on to produce his first major collection for Fashion Week in March 1985. From being allowed to present tea-stained muslin, crushed silks with walking sticks and wigs at College, he has progressed to smashed glasses, tadpoles in jars, alarm clocks on hats and grass through the hair, as added accessories for his recent Pillar Hall Show.

Meanwhile, at the Royal College of Art, fashion at M.A. level has taken on a far more serious note. There is still a certain amount of wit, but here the fashion department works with the 3.D course to present a stage and set, especially designed for the clothes to be shown on. This signifies a strong direction from the students' work because it emphasises their clothes in a different manner to the normal runway structure. The majority of models are sent out with a uniform look. Recent sets have included electronic, electric-lit heads, scaf-folding fire escape ladders and huge screens magnifying the models as they leave and enter the stage. The students here tend to follow the trail abroad, where they are immediately scooped up for jobs. Because of the emphasis on reality, the designs are less indi-dual and more disciplined. The

● Roland Klein, original designer sketch, Autumn '85

students, rather than establishing their own businesses, are regularly employed with top designer positions. Shown here is the work of David Backhorse who went on to work with Roland Klein.

● Roland Klein, catwalk reality, Autumn/Winter '85

ROLAND KLEIN

This designer is mainly known for his style and co-ordination in contemporary clothes. His collection does not only mix and match but also lasts. After the cloth is ordered and worked out into its fabric groups, each range is individually considered. For the recent March '85 showing of his Autumn/Winter collection, flower and checks were mixed, to stripes with plains and gloss with matt in contrasting colours. When the designer views each section of the range separately one theme should

● Roland Klein, catwalk reality, Autumn/Winter '85

not appear to be weaker than the others. When the collection is almost completed, the concept of showing it on a catwalk is arranged. Each model girl was booked for having the same look, with scraped

back hair and the same colour red lipstick – a strong feature as one face merged with another and did not overpower the clothes. To create a feeling of space the runway was extended, almost filling one end of the room to the other in length. There were hardly any centre front seats, instead the audience viewed the clothes from the left and right, almost like being round a boxing ring. The models stormed or glided down the catwalk from a tunnel effect at the end. From a gap in the distance they came towards you and the power of the colour hit you immediately. The buyers could see the clothes and immediately knew how and where they would sell, the press could understand the look. The show proved a success.

● Wendy Dagworthy, the space to be filled

WENDY DAGWORTHY

The first so-called 'continuous' show I ever staged was with this designer. We had two weeks to work together and the show was almost ready to stage. The collection from beginning to end involved the same fabric choice and the same shapes, repeated in a mass of variations. The coats, jackets, trousers, dresses, shirts, waistcoats, leggings, vests, t-shirts, were all layered on top of each other in a multitude of ways. Therefore, it seemed best to show the audience the collection in one go, from beginning to end without any break. The models danced up and down the catwalk in an entertaining way, getting off on the music, finding each other along the run-

● Wendy Dagworthy, models walk on by, Autumn/Winter Men's Wear '85

way, making a friend and having a dance. The clothes looked like fun things to wear. Since then, October 1983, the concept for showing this collection has developed. The models are now joined into small tribes – the blonde girls, the dark girls and the men. They enter the stage as a co-ordinated unit and then break apart to mix and match with other partners to show how the clothes can be worn by a whole population. The Russian clockwork doll and soldier look for Autumn/Winter '85 was shown in a mechanical manner. Another Wendy Dagworthy show, loved by the

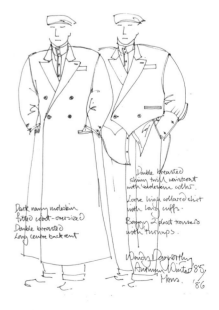
● Wendy Dagworthy, original designer sketch, Autumn/Winter Men's Wear '85

BodyMap

Genethlialogia

Phyfiog...mia.

Prophetia

Geomantia

Pyramidumicierna

Geomantia

presents
the
HALF

audience. Stirrup leggings in knits were worn with contrasting socks in bold primary colours and the women wore large men's walking shoes. The models in their huge frock coats clomped along and created an image unseen elsewhere.

BODYMAP

This rapidly expanding new company, presented their half-world collection in March '85. The toast of 1984, have used incredibly innovative runway ideas. The whole family have worn the clothes on the catwalk including mums, cousins, nephews and nieces as well as performers, pop-stars, dancers and singers. The

● BodyMap, Men's Wear, Half-World Collection, Autumn/Winter '85

models have been the minority in the crowd. From the idea of re-moving the backwall of the cat-walk one season, to reveal all of the backstage scenes to the audi-ence, this time round the designers presented their clothes in a semi demi-couture manner. Crochet knits almost painted onto the body made the models look like poodles, covered in reversible crushed nylon in sherbert colours. The main accessory this season were plastic globes carried by the models, dis-playing numbers. Slightly off-beat, the numbers were not in sequence, neither were the clothes. However, once the models entered the stage and formed into a straight line, it was obvious to see how the ranges

had been engineered. It was fas-cinating to see how separate the performers could look in their own right. A clever concept and a directional move-on from the continuous way that designers have shown their clothes in the past. One of the stronger areas was perhaps their American stretch denim for the U.S.A. market covered in contrasting ruffles and gold fringe braiding. With com-mentary from either Helen Terry or their hairdresser, the designers announce to the world what their collection is about.

● Bernstock-Speirs, original designer sketch and show invitation, Autumn/Winter '85

BERNSTOCK & SPEIRS

Perhaps from the March 1985 season this is one company who will go on to be recognised for changing the face of fashion. Starting out as accessory designers, developing the infamous topless knitted hat, they have now gone on to develop exclusive clothing ideas in their very own personal way. Their use of colour tones and muted shades, either vegetable, metal, sludge or just plain dark, emphasises the shape of the gar-ments to the best of their advantage.

The inspiration for this collection was international. The models had their faces painted like gypsies but looked more like sun-tanned South American ladies. The majority of hats were bowlers, in bright velvet colours and were worn on top of cloth wigs slightly 'Avengers' style. The garments ranged from American cut macs to British style riding-wrap skirts and street-belted trousers. A model's face and hair was never fully revealed – they were always covered in some form of an accessory. They hit the stage in six or eight, to a strobe effect – walking in slow-motion which gave the effect of a time-warp. The mixture of models parading the clothes gave the

● Bernstock-Speirs, Shotgun Dressing on the catwalk, Autumn/Winter '85

show a variety of entertainment. The face of fashion here proved to look extremely foreign and it is hard to believe that both the designers are British and have been working together in this country for some time.

JEAN MUIR

A major institution of British fashion, and my major delight for 1985, was to work with this de-signer on the presentation of her Autumn/Winter '85 collection. For the first time I was able to work on a range of clothes where every garment was perfect. For this show there was no catwalk. It is in the Bruton Place showroom, and one model is sent out at a time to an audience seated on red velvet chairs. The atmosphere is like an examination – nothing can afford to go wrong. But watching the way this designer works, there is no reason why anything should fail. Each garment is carefully considered, excellently cut, and in a choice of fabric which is so luxurious everyone would be willing to wear it. The models, interestingly enough are allowed to do their own hair and make-up. They are not dictated to by artists who have their own seasonal look in mind. They do whatever they feel suits their faces best, and because of that enter the audience in a relaxed manner, feeling proud to show off their natural beauty. The music

● Jean Muir brights receive the same treatment, Spring/Summer '85

RETAIL

As mentioned earlier, it is now the vogue for the High Street shops and manufacturers to present their ranges in a fashion show, mainly aimed at the Press so that they will be able to use the departments merchandise, alongside a designer's merchandise in any editorial work they will be doing in the future. This obviously enables the public to see that they can dress in next season's look for discount prices, as well as high fashion prices. Most of the department stores tend to work in a block manner. They organise their major themes for each season and divide them and punctuate them into

sections for fabric and styling. Whether it be sportswear, men's wear, or evening wear, a lot of clothes shown do tend to follow en suite from the designer collections shown in the previous season.

For major advertising campaigns, by using young photographers, stylists and a different form of model, or from new shop window display concepts by using the open French way of window dressing, the High Street shop is almost on par with the Fashion Week collections. From Marks & Spencer's for example one is able to buy for this Spring/Summer the same cotton sweater in a variety of eighteen different colours, co-ordinated with Lacoste shirts and

● Marks & Spencer, pullover power, Spring/Summer '85

socks. This could be the monopoly over the high fashion designer collections. Not many of the British designers for example can produce the same garment in such a variety of shades, with the same quality control and make. It is for our retailers to streamline and change the face of fashion by the product they now supply.

INTERNATIONAL

During 1985 designers throughout the world have shown their collections in a multitude of ways, different to that of the British designers. Some of these could prove to be the new concept for collection showing. For example, Girbaud in Paris have recently

● Jean Muir, understated statement, Spring/Summer '85

does not interfere. It is basically piano instrumental, and hidden away in the background. There is a rhythm, but it does not overpower the clothes. The showroom is set with trees and flowers, and the wooden shutters are thrown open at the windows to reveal natural light. Chandeliers are turned off and the show begins. Because each outfit is so special one does not feel the need to see a line-up of six girls at a time to prove how worthy the clothes are. This lady, has obviously found the correct show format for her clothes. There is always something for everyone. It has proved to be one of Britain's best classics. The Miss Muir look is always something to be proud of.

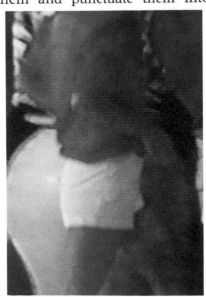
● Marks & Spencer, boys bare their legs, Spring/Summer '85

shown their collection alongside their exhibition stands. The company rents a space, builds a tent and houses inside it a canvas runway, clothes rails, smart desks, chairs, tables, and installs a video in every corner of the room to show the previous collection. Whilst one is waiting for the show to begin, you can either browse through the clothes, if you are the Press or place an order, if you are a buyer. Refreshments are available throughout the day. Models wander around aimlessly in the clothes and the casual air makes one feel at home. Suddenly, unannounced the lights will go on above the runway, the tent lights do not dim, and a model will appear to show the collection. The music and atmosphere is incredibly laid-back.

duced for the American markets. Norma Kamali and Stephen Sprouse are the two main new names who have revolutionised fashion in America. Sprouse for his extreme bright and fluorescent colours, very '60s influenced, has sent models out in wigs and comments have led to 'are they men or women?' Kamali has accepted the video format for her show and makes an advance tape of the collection, to launch on her viewing audience. That is then marketed throughout the world to all her suppliers and projected in the shop alongside the merchandise.

From all this it can be seen that a designer has a wide choice to decide which method of showing suits their range best. Backstage, is

● Plans from above, Mikel Rosen at work

● Dancers instead of models, Victoria & Albert Museum

If there happens to be a dog with one of the public and the dog decides to go on the catwalk, it is allowed to do so. If the models decide to walk in one's, two's or three's they are allowed to do so. The whole philosophy here is wearable, stylish, but extremely commercial – the company is doing well. Over the States, the American buyers throughout 1985 have taken most of their influence from British fashion. With the position of the dollar and the pound it has been good to export clothes from young British designers. The majority of American designers either show in the showroom format or in a hotel room in a lavish way. The models are normally extremely classic, and wear clothes in fabric exclusively pro-

where the catalyst for the future begins. A quick flash look of how a model may pose or use a certain garment can be the inspiration for the forthcoming season.

New messages can quickly be found in the haste of not having the time to correctly fasten a pair of braces and letting them conveniently hang loose over the trousers, or a skirt being too tight and therefore being allowed to be wrapped in folds around the hips. Consequently the new collections begin, giving new ideas for hair, make-up, staging, lights, music, models, dressers and show producers.

● Before the events

● Florizontal Men's Wear, Drapers Hall

38

MEDIA
MANNEQUIN

Reading between the seams

© Sascha · Photo by Richard Hopkins

© Joan Collins · Photo by David Bailey

© Gisela · Photo by Cloud Van Eck

IAIN R. WEBB

© Mannequins by Adel Rootstein, courtesy of Adel Rootstein

charmed she asked him to buy her three boas: black, white, and orange.

Monday, March 10.
The opening of the Rocky Horror Show at the Beautiful Belasco. Cabaret on Broadway, hopefully to stay. **Tim Curry**, the star, is brilliant, especailly when he sings "I'm Just a Transvestite-from Transexual Transylvania." He thinks he's doing Bette Davis but he's much more like Judy Garland, tortured with big shoulders. **Leo Lerman** was there for Vogue, and Diane von Furstenberg with **Yash Gabronski**, the Walter Cronkite of Italy, and **Silvana Magano** with her son **Federico di Laurentiis** and his Scandivian girlfriend **Mona**, who danced with **Ingrid Boulting** who danced with **Anjelica Huston**, who danced with Apolllonia von Ravenstein who danced with Sean Byrnes who danced with Pat Ast's furs. **Art Garfunkel** didn't dance and **Clive Barnes** didn't laugh once during the

Picture this if you can. A rather lucid boy of fourteen, torn apart by his preoccupation with puberty and pop music. The walls of his room are covered with high gloss oversized idols whose attractiveness is more a question of airbrush than birthright. There are magazines strewn across the floor, all opened to reveal page after page of perfectly groomed and excited looking models in all manner of glamour.

The boy eyes an article, and re-reads a line or two. It is filled with names of exotic sounding personalities, and stranger sounding possibilities. The boy is starry eyed. 'This is for me', he breathes as he pulls on the brightly coloured acrylic tank-top he blackmailed his mother to buy him, or cuts another ten inches or so from the hem of his pants in an effort to make himself 'fashionable'. 'One day . . . ' he dreams.

It is in fact Real Life.

I know. I was *that* boy.

The posters, magazines, photographs and cutely-cut interviews are the stuff dreams are made of. Built on. They are all lies.

It was a distressing realisation when I first got to be involved with fashion that things just weren't like that. I would have been fooling myself to believe so. But just who fools us? The media machine is a wickedly cruel machine. Unfeeling. Insensitive. It tells us things which *we* believe to be so, simply because of its age and assumed reverence.

'It's there in the papers – *must* be the truth.'

Don't believe a word. Media representations of life are no more accurate than some fairy's tales. As Art supposedly imitates life, so T.V. and film produce their own versions. More adaptation than imitation.

So where does this leave the business of Fashion? Itself an imaginary place where castles are built on thin air; thin values – and fat cheque books. How has the media dream treated those ordinary folk down on Fashion Farm? Answer is, quite badly.

T.V. has gone ape for fashion this year. Even everyday programmes. Day-in-the-life soap operas have introduced a little splash of colour and fabric into their midst.

Mike Baldwin's factory in *Coronation Street* (which previously 'ran up jeans') has been even more alive than Princess Diana's designers when it came to setting trends. In fact at one point it was almost possible to imagine a visit from the regal one herself, just so she could get her hands on one of those much coveted flying suits.

Yes, the big fashion story this year, in T.V. scriptwriters wardrobes anyhow, was the flying suits. As Vera Duckworth and Ivy Tilsley quibbled over who was to model the darned thing, so Mike wined and dined his new find, designer Christine Millward 'Gold dust, my dear.' . . . and another phone call had them begging for more. 'Imagine our flying suits in one of those boutiques in Carnaby Street', one of the girls mused. Spot on. Carnaby Street. The hub-bub of British fashion . . . A little nearer to the truth, if still no further from it, is Covent Garden, home of *Gems* Now we have it. Fashion has become public property, and so it must have its very own soap opera, all itself. Researched and advised by respected designer names, *Gems* storylines are based around a fashion company of the same name. It begins every programme with an endless stream of models strutting Covent Garden, followed closely by dolly-boy photographer who snaps every smile.

The script, however, has you squirming. So the story goes, someone actually spent weeks – months perhaps – at a well-known fashion company, listening and listing all

● Mile Baldwin talks taffeta with his top designer in *Coronation Street*

that went on. This then is the reason why almost every show (and it runs three times a week) begins or ends with characters repeating such lines: 'We went pretty big with the Americans – silk jersey dresses . . .'; 'does that skirt length bother you?'; or the gripping, 'to me pattern grading is just drawing on a piece of paper half an inch bigger all round . . . now that may be a simplistic view . . .'

Never a truer word.

It has since become a pass time for more aware designers to try and reintroduce these lines back into fashionable society . . . and

● *Coronation Street*, the flying suit phenomenon

● *Gems*, models set the pace in Covent Garden

so life imitates. In the same week that Zandra Rhodes had £250,000 worth of frothy chiffon stolen, 'Gems' also had a robbery. Six jackets went missing. These are probably already collectors items. Works of Art, as Zandra might say.

Gems has it all. The machinists are either young, unmarried and pregnant (naturally) or old and crabby; the photographer is an upper crust gigolo who carries his own camera always looking for a picture; the pattern cutter has a dubious sexual preference; and the designs are specially

created by the students at the Royal College of Art. It is missing one thing. Humour.

The bigger the screen, the bigger the horrors appear. *Mahogony* is possibly the most ludicrous and implausible 'Fashion film' ever made. It is even a ludicrous **film**. *Mahogony* stars Diana Ross, who plays the title role. The movie's press handouts tell us that. 'Diana portrays a world famous High Fashion model and designer in this dramatic international love story . . .'. Who Diana's part is based on has never been revealed, although I can think of more than one British designer who would like to be a model. None of them however would fit into the slinky,

outrageously camp gowns Ms. Ross wears throughout the film, although I suspect many of them have tried . . . eh, chaps? but back to the plot.

Diana, or *Mahogony* captivates an international jet-setter who will 'sponsor' her in her struggle for fame as a high fashion designer. Note that the term High Fashion is always used when it's in technicolor. Twice as bright, as are the aforementioned creations. The pressmen describe them so: 'A stunning group of Oriental inspired costumes personally designed by Diana Ross highlights a fashion show sequence.' These were not the work of students from the Royal College of Art.

● *Gems*, real life characters

● *Mahogany*, catwalk fantasy or freak show horror

Apart from spending her time being photographed in the streets by talented 'but tormented' Antony Perkins who 'opens the door for her modelling career', she also has time to lose not only Mr. Perkins but also her lover, Billy Dee Williams because he 'disapproves of her friends and exotic lifestyle in Rome'; and almost her own life in a near fatal car accident. Of course Ms. Ross is lucky enough to be aided to recovery by the international jet setter who will sponsor her career . . . etc., etc.

Mahogony. Dark, sensual, . . . and a . . . s(t)inker.

● Faye Dunaway keeping fit by taking pictures

● Diana Ross strutting it on the street in *Mahogany*

Blow-Up and *The Eyes of Laura Mars* both give us insights into the lives of top Fashion photographers, played respectively by David Hemmings and Faye Dunaway. Both become involved in murder mysteries, which is possibly not such a far-out idea as people might imagine as there are many, many people in the fashion business one would willingly murder.

However, *Blow-Up*'s portrayal of the fashion photographer as Jack the Lad – all East End and sports car, is no nearer to the truth than Laura Mars who is wrapped in all manner of designer dresses, and is

photographed photographing her dead-on-their-feet models wearing a skirt which has no shame, and a pair of shoes which have no centre of gravity. Even models find it difficult to walk in anything over four and a half inches high, let alone steady themselves whilst focusing in a position which would work up Jane Fonda.

The heels of Laura Mars' shoes are obviously the reason someone wants to kill her. An angry model perhaps, caught between the crossfire and camera shake? Another similarity the pair share is the exerting amounts of sex they indulge in. In *Blow-Up* the camera becomes David Hemmings phallus, and almost every photo session ends in an orgasm. This is *not* true. Orgasms come when the pictures have been developed, not when they are being taken. Then it is only headaches which fill the studios . . .

Funnier still is Fred Astaire acting as a photographer in *Funny Face*. It is he who shoots Audrey Hepburn to stardom as a model. However, both are upstaged by the perfectly wonderful portrayal of a Fashion Editor by Maggie Prescott. It is she who heads *Quality* magazine, and makes all the decisions. Girls are discarded; lives are ruined; the world changes colour all on her say so. 'Think Pink', she hollers, and everyone within spitting distance does. She is always

● *Blow-Up.* An orgy of falsehoods

● David Hemmings tries to focus

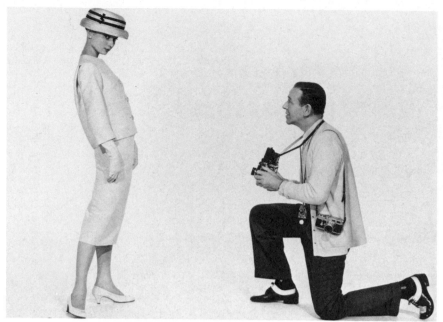

● Fred Astaire shows how to photograph a *Funny Face*

huddled around like the three witches in Macbeth. 'Hubble, bubble, toil and trouble.'

The trouble being that none of it was *for real*.

The 'team' were photographed all arriving at the same time – which *never* happens; the photographer and I worked as one, never stepping on each other's toes ('What in *these* heels?'); and *every-one* was pictured forever nodding approval. What it did not show was the days spent walking from store to store with bin-liners full of clothes, accessories, and shoes; endless phonecalls trying to cajole said stores into lending said clothes, accessories and shoes; egos at work and cameras not; the drink flowing as fast as the foul language; and

neatly dressed. Never a hair out of place, and always wearing a hat and/or gloves. She is constantly surrounded by a team of similarly attired young ladies who bow to her every whim.

'Dear quality magazine,

Re. The vacancy for Fashion Editor on your magazine.

I would very much like to be considered for the above position.'

If only life were really like that . . . but it isn't.

I recently experienced this for myself when I was featured on a BBC T.V. pop magazine show in

much the same role. Fashion Editor. The five minute film attempted (quite admirably) to show just what such a person does for a living. It featured frames filled with talk of 'free-form', and 'Beardsley'; the hairstylist giving an explanation as to what she was about to do to the models hair, which sounded more like the answer to an O-level paper: 'The length of a person's hair, and its meaning in modern society. Discuss?'; and the gathering to view a polaroid that had myself, the photographer and his assistant

● Models die for fashion in *The Eyes of Laura Mars*

creativity flowing even faster.

It was a deodorised version which reached the screen, but unfortunately it is that which some rather lucid fourteen year old may pin their dreams on. 'And now you know what a stylist does', the announcer proclaimed directly after the film.

Not what I do, you don't.

The scary thing is that it leaves you wondering just how much you can believe – of anything . . .

T.V.? Fashion? The Newspapers? The Nine O'clock News?

The boy has since grown up, and the tank-top has been pushed to the back of the wardrobe . . . for the moment.

● Maggie Prescott in *Funny Face*; not a bin liner in sight

● Thanks to Columbia, MGM/UA, Paramount
● Thanks to Transworld Feature Syndicate and Thames Television

DRESSING FOR ROYALTIES

"There's a brand new dance but I don't know its name"

(David Bowie – 'Fashion')

TOM WATKINS
NIKKI SLIGHT

47

Photo by: Anne Leibovitz

FACT: Before the '80s, pop stars were never particularly designer-conscious. Historically, the most potent pop fashions have always been inextricably linked to the youthquake of the moment; teds, mods, rockers, skinheads, punks – each had (and still have) their own musical mascots.

Yet Britain in 1985 is bereft of any one widely-adopted youth cult. Such trends reached their appropriate conclusion with punk – the only significant movement since that of those well-documented over made-up tarts the, New Romantics.

The media overkill which greeted New Romantic groups such as Visage, Duran Duran and Spandau Ballet in the late '70s coincided with the growing popularity of colour pop magazines such as *Smash Hits* and the sudden importance of the promo video. This was the launch pad which rocketed the contemporary western world into the throes of a pop-media explosion which is now fast approaching saturation point.

Britons today are exposed to so much, so quickly, that no sooner have you filled your head with £100 worth of synthetic tresses than some clever Boy George is telling you to cut them out. Then – six weeks post-scissors you spot Pete 'Boy' Burns on *Top Of The Pops*, growling from beneath the most magnificent mane you've ever witnessed.

Confused? Actually, no. The bulk of Britain's youth simply pick and choose. Pop style in '85 is dedicated to the same cult as the decade's fashion – the cult of the individual.

The massive multi-media exposure awaiting any '80s pop group has made image/individuality a crucial concern. It follows that many artists have therefore embarked upon that inevitable journey, the pursuit of fashion – some becoming so well clued-up as to leave shop assistants stuttering in their wake. This new pop/fashion empathy was marked by a bizzare celebration.

Dateline: London. Summer 1984. Pop discovers designer fashion. Correction – it discovers Katharine Hamnett and pronounces her style doyenne of the music business. Hit acts including Wham!, Duran Duran, The Thompson Twins and Spandau Ballet adopted Hamnett's crumpled combats with fervent enthusiasm – only to be outdone by the annual pop phenomenon, Frankie Goes To Hollywood, who (aided and abetted by XL), plagiarised the designer's ecological slogan t-shirts, substituting them for their own 'Frankie say' messages. In Britain, the latter proved to be the bigger sellers. Frankie agitprop writ large, proliferated at an almost nightmarish rate through every city in the country. Fascinating proof that when pop and fashion join forces, optimum exploitation may be achieved in little more than a fortnight.

The Frankies – or more specifically frontmen Paul Rutherford and Holly Johnson, are pop's most prolific designer clotheshorses since Bryan Ferry last strolled into the sunset in his Anthony Price. As the royalties for their mega-hit single 'Relax' rolled in, the duo dashed down South Molton Street and returned bedecked in Gaultier and Yamomoto. Their fashion sense even earned the pair four pages in British Vogue – Holly's Raleigh cycling cap being the only garment to bear a price tag of less than three figures. Evidently, the boys were doing what came naturally. Interviewer to Paul Rutherford: "What were you wearing before you could afford Katharine Hamnett shirts?" Answer: "Katharine Hamnett shirts."

The Frankies are stylish. So is mint-cool jazz singer Sade, American classic Bruce Springsteen, '50s retro trio Matt Bianco and the intriguing Annie Lennox of Eurythmics. Yet while the latter

● Frankie Goes To Hollywood

● Rose and Jill of Strawberry Switchblade went dotty and made all their own clothes

● Dead Or Alive wearing designer Dean Bright

exude an air of chic independence, '80s fashion has claimed a heavy toll of fatalities in the name of style.

The singularly unattractive brocade renaissance of Winter '84/85 sparked off a welter of gaudy waistcoats and fake pearls which ran the gamut of Duran Duran and The Thompson Twins before heaving to a graceless halt on the backs of Spandau Ballet – five so-called hip North London lads who should have known better.

While a number of artists continue to steal from the catwalk, those who develop their own look (albeit with a measure of guidance) seem to pack more punch. First chart newcomers to strike lucky in '85 were Glaswegian duo Strawberry Switchblade who exploded into the charts in a riot of polka dots which covered not only

● Alannah Currie of The Thompson Twins . . . wearing her socks on her head

their shoes, hair ribbons and flamenco dresses but also their guitars. A fortnight later the entire Switchblade wardrobe was spotted at Top Shop.

Hot on their heels came King – professing to represent a both musical and sartorial hybrid. All sported spray-painted Doc Marten boots and long locks while front-man Paul King favoured half-mast tartan suits and the rest threatened a tepid version of the New York Dolls meet Motorhead. Their highly successful (ie. distinctive) image was skilfully orchestrated by the band's whizz-kid manager Perry Haines, a former face about the capital's clubs who knows his way around a clothes rail.

And then there were Dead or Alive – last of the 'gender benders' Pete Burns as characterised by a mass of waist length black hair,

● First rate Doc Martin boot salesman Paul King of King

floor sweeping coats, wife, boyfriend, eyepatch and nosejob. 'The Deads' all-purple stage clothes were commissioned from rising young design talent Dean Bright who earlier, had been headhunted by David Bowie's stylists to clothe the hero for his 'Blue Jean' video. The Burns look embodied the last fading cries of London's glam rock revival. Satin and tat had blazed a tacky trail through the clubs but ultimately made small impression on the charts – despite the threatened resuscitation of '70s glam heroes The Sweet and the third coming of Gary Glitter – now registered as a listed building. The most convincing exponents of contemporary glam are, sur-

● Gary Glitter still piling it on in '85

prisingly, white soul/funksters ABC. Following their yet to be matched success of the early '80s, the band have now reappeared brilliantly transformed into cartoon caricatures by their newly-acquired 'percussionist' Eden, aka writer/club celebrity Fiona Russell Powell.

Across the pond the Americans have substituted hard-edged glam for sub-Dynasty glamour. A full-scale British invasion is now well under way with camped-up Regency buck Prince in the vanguard – one of the few American stars to emerge with any sense of style for many a month.

Following his Royal Badness over the Atlantic are a technicolour

army of artists united only by gender. Pop's new wave of female stars arrive armed with a new-found strength and dressed to kill. Each has their own highly individual look and include traditionally vamped-up starlet

● World megastar Prince, in a vintage trash glamour ensemble

Madonna, 'new wave Betty Boop' Cyndi Lauper, Chaka Khan, Pat Benatar and Prince protégées Sheila E and Apollonia 6. Without a single designer label between them, Lauper and Madonna have opted for the mix and mismatch thrift-shop approach to dressing, and, laden with A LOT OF JEWELLERY, look very Italian punkette with something here, there and everywhere to delight/offend anyone.

Although Madonna claims she's 'Like A Virgin', these girls are not sex, they are nobody's sex objects. Together they represent the most assertive collection of female role models ever witnessed. They are refreshing by virtue of the sheer variety of their respective images. Godmother of them all is the incandescent Tina Turner who shimmied her way through a recent TV awards bash in a red sequinned backless mini-dress and little else. 'Marvellous for her

● The boy next door plays it safe, Paul Young

age', but fashionable it wasn't. She should worry . . . confidence spells style with a capital S.

British girls are also having a field day. Most notably Alison Moyet – a fan of designers Wendy Dagworthy and Betty Jackson –

and, darling of the upwardly mobile, that modern classic, Sade. Considering the aforementioned speed of media overkill – which allows artists little space for improvement and consolidation – it is not surprising that many decide to base their wardrobes upon the styles of past decades. This hefty slice of the British pop circus includes Matt Bianco, The Big Sound Authority and The Style Council as well as Sade. All of them *Face* readers, they apparently set themselves 'behind' and so therefore 'above' fashion.

While all this sounds pretty dull (ie. very safe) there is evidently something to be said (ie. chart returns) for the above approach.

● Howard Jones, the long and the short of it

Thankfully, should variety be the spice of life, then there are many more who project a discernable pop 'image' whilst apparently never giving style a second thought. All human life is here – from the bland Mr Nice Guys such as Howard Jones and Nik Kershaw to the boys and girls next door – Paul Young and Hazell Dean. If this is difficult to fathom, then it is worth remembering that pop music is now over thirty years old and therefore a lot more people like it than ever before. Many over-thirties love Howard Jones and his dangerous haircut.

It is further evident that the British public considers nothing more stylish than an English

Eccentric. At time of writing, the eccentric's crown rests precariously upon the wanton intellectual head of one Steven Morrissey, lead singer of band The Smiths. An intriguing latter-day Hamlet – his Evans outsize blouse all unbutton'd and his Levis all unkempt – Morrissey, is an irresistible mixture of contradictions – all dubious sexuality and crypitc one-liners. Confusion (sometimes) keeps him locked in his room for hours and hours – 'I would go out tonight, but I haven't got a stitch to wear', (The Smiths – This Charming Man). His is the familiar song of the angst-ridden sixth former, many of whom are reported to have dropped

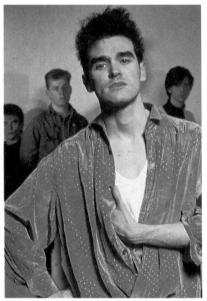

● The Smiths lead singer Morrissey strikes a Napoleonic pose on an Evans outsize blouse

their W.H. Audens and plundered their Mum's wardrobes on just one hearing.

To win his title, Morrissey deposed heavyweight champion Boy George who said too much too soon and massacred his mystique. Expect a long silence followed by a spectacular comeback from the Boy who definitely knows his BodyMap from his Wendy Dagworthy.

As for future pop trends, XL predicts more hetero sex – Andrew Ridgely, unmarried Durans and Madonna – more midriffs (Morrissey and Madonna), more pop divorces parading through the tabloids (a silver disc spells wedded bliss was last year's thing) and

● Shades of Marilyn (Monroe) American pop goddess Madonna. Photo by: Stephen Meisel

● Boy George dressed down. Try as they might, they just couldn't upstage him! Photo by: Devon Agency

● Fringe benefits for new EMI signings Spelt Like This

more kiss and tell John Blake at the *Daily Mirror* or Martin Dunn at the *Sun* or Rick Sky at the *Daily Star*. Only a decade or so overdue, Fleet Street has just discovered pop music, all of which augurs extremely well for the promotion of pop fashion. There will be more alcohol and boasting and less modesty and hard drugs. All talk of drugs will be considered extremely bad styling, closely followed by any discussion of male homo-sexuality. Boys will be boys and no questions asked.

As for the names to watch, XL's money is on Spelt Like This – a young, free and damned sexy pop group – along with The Pet Shop

● Wise blood looks for new blood Pet Shop Boys

Boys who make a more eclectic pop music and are downright sinister. Spelt Like This spell energy and fun and dress accordingly in an amalgamation of classic rock denims and neo-classic fringing. The Pet Shop Boys look as if they're definitely up to something and their dress suggests a dark, over-powering shadyness.

The best pop stylists simply emphasise the exsisting qualities of a band to their best advantage. Designer clothes never got a talentless band anywhere. Those who are talented and inherently stylish are truly the gifted. Fact.

FIRST IN: FIRST OUT

How does it feel to be one of the Beautiful People

  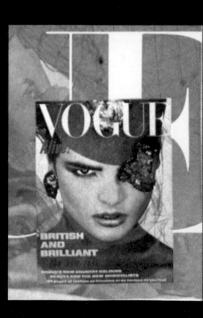

PAUL MORLEY

REPLIES: As if something has happened. By being asked to reply... ONE IS FORCED TO MAKE SOMETHING HAPPEN. One is forced to soothe the nerves.

TURN TO PAGE 22

LIES

It is the problem of how to steer between the rocks of discomfort and the sandbanks of looking a joke. It is the problem of how to be individual without being funny.

HISTORY

Other people in their time have worn odd clothes. Lord Byron, when he proceeded to liberate Greece, designed for himself a little Hussar uniform of green cloth with white frogs and tags. On top of this fussy little jacket he had meant to wear a huge helmet with a horse hair plume, such as one sees in heroic representations of the siege of Troy. But people laughed at his hat, and he put it back again in its pink bandbox. It can be seen today in his bedroom at Newstead.

LADIES HEAD-DRESS

Perhaps the *now* has been made notable by HATS. Is that how the moment will be recalled? There could be something to say about this. I will take the view – forcing something to happen, being bright and petulant – that I don't like hats. Let's suppose that it is impossible to add anything that can be ornamental to what is already a masterpiece of nature. *THE* masterpiece of nature. Describe it thus . . . 'the head has the most beautiful appearance, as well as the highest station, in a human figure. Nature has laid out all her heart and art in beautifying the face: she has touched it with vermillion, planted in it a double row of ivory, made it the seat of smiles and blushes, lightened it up and enlivened it with the brightness of the eyes, hung it on each side with curious organs of sense, given it airs and graces that cannot be described, and surrounded it with such a flowing shade of hair as sets all its beauties in the most agreeable light. In short, she seems to have designed the head as the cupola to the most glorious of her works: and when we load it with a pile of supernumerary ornaments, we destroy the symmetry of the human figure, and foolishly contrive to call off the eye from great and real beauties, to childish gew-gaws, ribands and bone lace. So much for hats.

FANS

Did fans make a comeback? If they did then perhaps young people today are more sophisticated than I would have been thinking . . . because to handle a fan is not at all a simple exercise. There is an infinite variety of motions to be made use of in the flutter of a fan. There is the angry flutter, the modest flutter, the timorous flutter, the confused flutter, the merry flutter and the amorous flutter. Not to be tedious, there is scarce any emotion in the mind which does not produce a suitable agitation in the fan. A fan is either a prude or coquette according to the nature of the person who bears it. What a useful thing!

The human face alvine

FOOD

It became the time when for many who'd never thought of it before, food became a thing not to treat with flippancy. In food, as in many things, the surprising is delightful providing that it is not overdone. Like all events which gratify the senses, food should be approached anxiously though calmly . . . coffee was drunk this year. And of course English coffee, as ladled out to the public, is not as good as that obtained in Austria or in France. For some there was the first fresh asparagus . . . but then, how quickly do such things pass out of our lives!

I am waiting for my soup.

UNFOOD

The dislike which France bore for 'England food' can now be summed up in two words of withering reproach: Bernard Matthews. His evil animal pulp symbolises the surrender to vulgarity that in many ways was the year as it was. The year saw widespread rejection of experience. And of course the only form of vulgarity which really matters is that form which leads its victims to reject experience.

THE SMALL IRRITATIONS IN LIFE

What really happened can be conjured up through one list: the Weetabix figures, through which one could see the complete condescending look at all things moving from a (aggression) to b (breakdance) to c (computers) and see how hard the language has been Smash Hit; the me of Maxwell; morning television idiot costumes; sarcasm; collective guilt removed by acts of illuminated generosity; the gravitation towards catastrophe.

From d (daft) to e (extravagance) to f (fun, with all its flat pretence) to . . . the idea of newness itself. What flashes thus, while serence contemplation now attains merely the socially pre-formed plaster cast of things, is itself repetition. The new, sought for its own sake, a kind of laboratory product, petrified into a conceptual scheme, becomes in its sudden apparition a compulsive return of the old . . .

NOW

Poe's allegory of the 'novel' is that of the breathlessly spinning yet in a sense stationary movement of the helpless boat in the eye of the maelstrom. ('New-ness' in collective form, well, it is in fact a stimulating and paralysing narcotic extract boiled out of external life . . .)

THEN

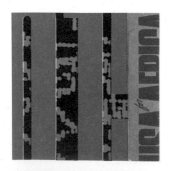

To be asked to reply . . . when all it has been is a bit of bits and pieces, more additions to the catalogue, more traits of fetishism, and the hoarding, plus some signs of advanced taste . . . For me the year could have been six pieces of coloured chalk; a smooth long nosed mask spied in a corner shop in Venice; Jeffrey Barnard's 'Low Life' column in *The Spectator*; Brain Hayes still 'speaking of things' on the London Broadcasting Company; Napa Valley Brut; Palamo Picasso's Silver Scribbles; Waterford Crystal; breathing . . . But does this make an impression? To be asked to reply is to be asked to take refuge, to make *the* impression, to sort it out, to take it apart, to deny the repetition – after a fashion. At first sight what could be more simple than being asked to reply? The simple answer is that the dominant factors have been haste, nervousness and restlessness. These things do not belong in the catalogues 'list of protection' and these things cannot be photographed. To reply properly is to tumble away from the specific, to chuck up for no reason the bits of bits and pieces. Nothing has happened that can't be put down to just a load more attempts to get worked up about looks, Tuesday, profit, rapture, cosmetics, absence, egotism and superstition. Something happens. It is photographed. It has happened. Read all *about* it. Copy it. Fill the gap. Confess. It is the problem of appearing ignorant, or clueless: the thought of particular indelicacies, micro-organisms of wrongdoing, unnoticed perhaps by anyone else; such trifles as the wrong colour and the wrong year and the wrong size can fill the delinquent with unconquerable remorse and a passionately bad conscience, and on occasion with such burning shame that he shrinks from confessing them even to himself. Or so we are led to believe. Faced with such bits and pieces of pieces there are perhaps only five replies.

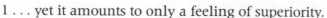

1 . . . yet it amounts to only a feeling of superiority.
2 . . . Blank faced seriousness and pseudo-activity hold sway.
3 . . . one fears missing the bus and bringing on oneself the vengeance of the collective.
4 . . . Anyone who wants to move with the times is not allowed to be different.
5 . . . There is something repulsive, yet to a certain degree rational, about the prestige gained by those who can present themselves as such important people that they have to be on the spot everywhere.

QUESTIONS TO ASK HAMNETT AND J.P.G. AND WHOEVER ELSE YOU THINK

Do you merely pander to luxuriously narcissistic worries?
Is what we have here a representation of the barbaric success-religion of the now?
What is the goal of an emancipated society?
Are you just helping to kill time?
Do you blush?
How would you define 'exposing yourself to ridicule'?
Isn't to convey 'a message' simply to escape?
What is envy?
Do you always know what to expect?
Are you trying to mark the individuals who wear your clothes?
At first sight, what could be more simple?
Define temptation.

TAKE IT EASY

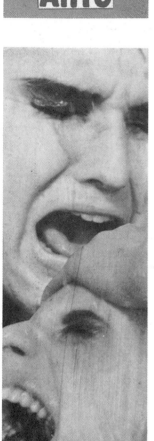

One is just too stupid, too old fashioned, one simply can't keep up. If the relation has grown sterile, it should be broken off. It is the problem of how not to feel cursed. A problem of maintaining tender concern. What has happened does not merely touch on language, but has happened within it. There is a sixth reply: cultivated superior trash. It's been another year in the 20th century. Some forms have decayed; some new things have been made up. Another reply! It's all about the appearance of happiness, and it's about time. You can tell by the photographs: the people either look too happy or too miserable. Too much.

FINALE

But after the age, let us say, of twenty-seven there are times when that strap –the one that holds the waistcoat at the back – is released or loosened. It is a terrible moment for any man when he catches himself loosening his strap. It marks the second stage in the grim process from elegance to comfort. Oh, some advice. Never take any exercise. Exercise develops muscles and once muscles have been developed they have to be banged to prevent them turning into fat. It is extremely painful to be banged. When young, always have your clothes made too large for you. This allows for development. Concentrate on colour rather than on shape. Colour can be bought in any shop. Be very successful in your public life. Fame, more than anything else, enables one to wear comfortable and even becoming clothes.

AND YET

. . . and yet it is all very difficult. You see, I have said very little about clothes because they do not interest me. Elbows do. And soup. And what can be done to skin.

REPLY

Noel Coward was right. The only proper reply is: 'White'.

Skin Care	
Lilac Hand Lotion	120ml
Lilac Cleansing Cream	50ml
Sunflower & Wheat Cream	50g
Enriched Moisturising Cream	50g
Avocado Moisturiser	120ml
Cucumber Cleansing Milk	120ml
Rose Petal Skin Freshener	120ml
Cream Face Mask	100ml
Scrub Cream	120ml

CLUBBED TO DEATH

Why be In when you could be Out

VAUGHAN TOULOUSE

All photos by Adam Read

LEIGH

Leigh shares an 11th floor council flat in Aldgate with Trojan, 'another boy'. He spends his days designing clothes and nights out on the town, a seasoned club going professional. The designs that attract the most attention at the clubs are the ones that will eventually find their way into his collections. He tells me he is 'unusual', in that he is 'Australian born'!

Taboo is the Thursday night weekly he co-runs with Tony whose idea it was to go out one afternoon in search of the perfect night-spot. They wound up the search on finding Maximus in Leicester Square 'it reminded me of SATURDAY NIGHT FEVER, a ceiling of flashing lights with a dance floor to match, plus liquid lights, separate wine, cocktail and spirits bars, it was like the Palace condensed into an area with enough room for 500 people'.

The same spot now houses Christians' 'Alphabet City' on a Tuesday fortnightly basis. 'The management suited the place nicely too, but I went straight to meet them and left all the talking to Tony then I turned up on the opening night with my new crushed rice crispy scabs look and told them I was the doorman. I think they were quite taken aback. Now I leave the door up to Tony and go downstairs and get pissed.

'Because I'm an outsider it's awkward to say whether I like it or not. I don't like it to be posey, it's just good fun, people running around being pissed. I like the mixture of trendies and medallion men who I openly encourage to come in, so it's not too homogenous, though they never seem to stay long once I start talking to them. I wonder why? DJs Jeffrey and Rachel play a complete mixture of Hi Energy, Blondie, Bucks Fizz, a lot of top twenty sounds, anything really.

'I go to most places. Total Fashion Victims, (Stephen Linard's, Wag, Tuesday nights), is improving, Do Do's, The Kit Kat Club and The Cozy in Berwick Street that's an after hours place in Berwick Street. It's like a front room, free to get in and a pound a drink until 6.00am.'

Leigh wears his own designs always, currently a collection of exaggerated shouldered suits, cut above the knee in checked worsted with spots and stripes, polka dotted silk scarves and matching stencilled face and neck, shorts and knee length socks, topped off with blue rinse granny wigs.

'I wouldn't wear other people's clothes I avoid them because I like to make my own statement and not imitate other people. I do like Vivienne Westwood, some BodyMap and Galliano, but I usually have intense fads for four months and saturate myself with one particular idea till I get so sick of it I just want to go and do the exact opposite.

'I'm not serious or precious about my look, it's just fun. I find it difficult to look after my clothes, I always seem to come home to discover a mass of cigarette burns, beer stains and scuffed shoes. I seem to be continuously falling over.'

MATT

A stone's throw away from the Fitzroy public house, just off Tottenham Court Road, lives Matt and his mate Paul, percussionist of up and coming Expresso 7. Matt DJ's his spare time away, mainly at Warehouse parties, and joins your humble narrator at Do Do's and the Wag, (Saturdays). Collects '50s/'60s cult teenage paperbacks, mainly for the covers, (his favourite is Hal Elisson's A NEST OF FEAR), and contemporary objects of the same period, 'anything that takes my fancy'. Records too, he has an impressive library of American Doo Wop singles, but goes for most music types from the '40s to present day, original copies and sleeves preferred.

Spends Friday nights at the Sol y Sombra, 'whenever I can get in. It gets well packed really quickly and I hate queuing to get in. The wallies usually get there really early and fill the place up. It's small close atmosphere reminds me of the Beat Route a few years ago, good mix of people, not too posey or pretentious, the music is danceable jazz, r'n'b and latin, nice for a change, you know, plus I only live around the corner – it's handy!

'I wear smart classic men's designs, original white dress shirts, Tootal scarves or cravats, loose cut pleated waist trousers and a '50s American summer jacket or big black wool coat, wide lapels, below knee length. I like the styles of '30s Hollywood, David Niven always looked the part. I don't like modern designers, any of them, try too hard to be different, end up looking totally uncool. The FACE fashion followers make me laugh, I think the individual should always dress for himself and even these days one should try to be in continual pursuit of good times.'

JUNE

June Lawrence, the lead vocalist of Brilliant, shares a Hampstead basement pad with Kate, the lead vocalist of Dream Academy and Spot The Cat. When she and Kate aren't hollering around the house June spends the majority of her waking hours writing (songs) and drawing. Nights she can be found prowling the Heath and Sunday afternoons are reserved for playing baseball with the 'Regents Park Seals', 'nothing too serious'. She occasionally permits herself session singing work for insights into other music and because it 'helps inspirationally'.

The Wag, formally the Whiskey A Go Go, is situated at the lower end of Wardour Street between Soho and Piccadilly. It's a small intimate affair, every night is given over to a different music form and a selection of top club jocks. Mondays it's the Jazz Room hosted by Paul Murphy and featuring live acts; Thurdays, introduces up and coming live P.A.'s; Tuesdays it's Total Fashion Victims – get there early to check Julia's odd ball trash pop and disc spin; and so on nightly until 4am Saturday morning; Sunday is a night of rest.

'The intimacy of it is cozy, I know a lot of the regulars and that, it's like a gathering in your front room. I don't think I'm typical of the general Wag goer, but I like it down there, especially at weekends, on average I suppose I'll know about a quarter of the people there so I don't mind dropping in on my own. I like the usual things, you know getting pissed, dancing if the sounds are right, I like classic disco hits, that sort of thing. Apart from the Wag, I only really go to Do Do's and parties anywhere.

'As for clothes, I dress for comfort, for myself rather than for your actual fashion reasons. Simple, plain outfits, not necessarily designer labels unless it's something I really need. Accessories are a must too, a little bit of jewellery never goes amiss. I was talking to Kate the other day whilst browsing through Marie Claire and she said 'I wish high heels would come back into fashion'. I had a real go at her, that's the sort of attitude I don't like, it's like if you don't fit into a particular stereotype you must be a freak or something, people who judge you by what you wear and form opinions of you from your look make me sick.

'I love '40s and early '50s styles. Schiaparelli period I collect fashion mags, newspapers and memorabilia from that time (born too late!). My advice to you girls is that you can never be without your little black dress.'

ADAM

Currently residing in a seedy West London vicarage 'full of screamers'. Adam studies textiles in a central London college and spends the remainder of his time taking 'photos by the million', mainly of drag queens for some reason. Drinks Pils to excess, his favourite haunt is Movements at the Bell in Kings Cross on Sunday nights.

'It's the same mix of faces every week and the fact that it takes place on a Sunday makes it very relaxing after tea at the vicarage, people don't seem to be only out to get pissed up, probably they are still nursing that Saturday night hangover. It's a nice place to socialise and although it's just a big pub it's like a cross between a pub and a club, it's got a dance-floor. The music's a mixture of white dance records and heavy black disco, it's the only place I know where you get to hear stuff like Severed Heads and the Smiths, most of the sounds I don't recognise, it's just like having a beat box in the corner. The geezers are usually quite bona too, good for a pull, I'll say no more than that! I go to Taboo, the Asylum and Do Do's – nice and mixed, I like a few girls around, can't stand places full of clones.

'The general scene can be a bit shut off, a lot of people are too concerned with what everybody else thinks and wears and as to whether you're 'in' or not. I'm just 'out' for a good time.

'Denim is my sort of gear, it's casual, good for walking around in, Levi's are always fashionable and always unfashionable if you know what I mean? It's a good turn on faded and ripped it just looks good, on other people anyway! I've got a pretty basic wardrobe, 'cos I'm a poor student. I'd wear sharp cut suits as well if I was in pocket, Italian early '60s. I also like Leigh Bowery's designs, not for myself, but he's so unrestricted it's like taking the piss out of clothes, doing opposites. I'll stick with Levi Strauss though, with D.M.s or brouges always worn in, second hand rose style.'

STEVE

Hailing from the 'coolest' part of town, South East London born and bred, Steve lives with his Mum and Dad and brothers in a firm family unit. He's obsessed with his music, drumming. Currently working with the Style Council, 'though any situation that requires care, feel, groove and an upfront back beat will do nicely, time permitting'. He's a 19 year old jazz maniac and goes to Ronnie Scotts Club in Frith Street, where he reckons the highlights over the past 12 months have been Nina Simone, Art Blakey and Elvin Jones. Has time to practise Kung Fu and 'follows the fortunes' of Charlton Athletic A.F.C. on the side.

'Ronnies is one of the few clubs you get to hear good live music, variety and see musicians who're still taking chances. It's small and informal so the atmosphere is happening and I like to watch people's reactions from the music, getting off on the set rather than getting wrecked at the bar, the drinks are too dear for that anyway.

'I go to a few disco club places as well. You know, the Sol y Sombra, Busbys some nights, the Wag and the Frog and Bucket in Maidstone is well 'ard!

'I think style is the main thing. Fashion is for the mincers of South Molton Street, men and women'.

Wears: 'Ice blue jeans with sharp creases is my style, highly polished D.M. shoes or Nike trainers when I'm working. Tennis shirts always buttoned up, names and labels are irrelevant. Traces of be bop, dark blue beret is the only head gear. Cliff Richard circa the YOUNG ONES, what a geezer! And Alex in CLOCKWORK ORANGE, Audrey Hepburn in BREAKFAST AT TIFFANYS I think it was. Who else is there? Art Blakey he's inspiration and Billy Bragg, love it, he wears Marks & Spencer sweaters and hush puppies, he's cool. I just don't like flares, and gender benders are boring. I hated the '70s, posers, ponces and pushers. 90% of Americans just have no style whatsoever. I don't like the crowd who go to Ronnie Scotts to eat rather than for the music you might as well go to Guggenheims. Ban the bomb . . . '

JANE

Jane has the attic flat of an Edwardian house in North Islington to herself. She works in the newsroom of a Holborn Publishers where she cycles to and from work 'if the weather's sunny'. Originally from Gosport in Hampshire, she made the move to London for her job nearly four years ago, but frequently returns home for weekends and holidays. Most evenings are spent making patchwork quilts and cushions, 'bit of dressmaking, that sort of thing'.

Occasionally she has a stall in Camden Market selling her wares. Listens to Bob Dylan 'but I'm not a hippy', and borrows records from friends to tape, 'without permission, do you think I'll be found out?'.

'I liked going to the Camden Palace until recently, the music's terribly boring there. Tuesday's I usually end up going to the Hippodrome on the spur of the moment, from the wine bar with a few friends. I don't think I've ever actually planned to go there, but I tend to end up there about once a week. The music makes the disco I always think, it's very poppy and danceable, a lot of current chart hits, I like dancing depending on what sort of mood I'm in. Weekdays are the best, weekends are just too busy, hot and uncomfortable, despite being so large inside. I suppose a lot of tourists come out at weekends, not that I mind, but when you can't breathe it must be time to go!

'Personally, I like to wear my own clothes. I pinch ideas from magazines, make up my own patterns, it's quite simple really. Joseph is my favourite if I'm buying. I could spend hours trying things on in Pour la Maison. I find muted subtle colours suit me best, I dislike shocking pinks, flouresent and shiny things. Cotton is very nice to work with, comfortable to wear. I steer clear of satin, lace, rubber, that sort of thing. I go for plain shoes too, flat soled Ravels, Russell and Bromley, they're my favourites, and jewellery – usually inexpensive junk, old silver, large earrings. Have you seen those silly girls who work in those fairy costumes at the Hippodrome – how embarrassing!'

MONICA CHONG

Born in Hong Kong, Monica Chong came to London to study fashion at the Chelsea College of Art in 1974. On completing her course, she worked at Browns in South Molton Street for six months before starting a personal collection, working with positive, strong colours, 'blacks, greys and reds', experimenting with her own ideas. Known for her black dresses, she sells to the upmarket end of the line. Into camp, fun, '50s and '60s influenced, they are flattering but comfortable. 'My main buyers are old ladies but I do get working girls ringing me up in search of something special at discount prices.'

Her designs, she informs me, 'suit chunky jewellery they tend to be basic therefore able to build on for individuality'. She collects old jewellery, Fonno Sette, plates and furniture, cabinets that are built on famous building designs for instance. She also likes to entertain the odd dinner party 'now and then'.

'I love White Trash, everyone I like seems to go there, it's got real club atmosphere, no disco pretensions. It closed just recently, that's a shame, but it was fun for a couple of years.' White Trash was once Philip Sallon's infamous Planets where George O'Dowd span the discs. More recently the Dencil Williams/Paul Bernstock hosted White Trash has finally had its day, soon to be replaced no doubt by another Saturday night spot and new clientele. No details as I write, but it is excellently placed just off the heart of Piccadilly for, someone with a fresh approach!

'The whole musical spectrum seems to be covered, (by the DJ's Boo and Pete Barrett), not the sort of thing I'd play at home, but it feels right there, I can't name records, I'm not a music expert. It's nice and small and there don't seem to be many clubs where a girl can march in without an escort and feel at ease. The bouncers annoy me, I hate being searched by male bouncers, why not get a girl to do the job? That time there were the stabbings there, it put me off going out for a long time, those types should never have got in in the first place, real ex-army thugs, five or six people were knived that night. Frightening.

'For myself, I wear black dresses or well tailored suits, very neat. I work out every day, (I passed comment on Monica's slim shape), but I love champagne, smoke occasionally, so if I find myself indulging heavily one night, I make up for it by working out an extra half hour the following day. My favourite designers are: dead ones – Schiaparelli, Chanel; living – Karl Lagerfeld, he's very witty with definite quality, Gaultier, the most important designer of the '80s, and Yohji, I like his men's wear, I adore little details that have a purpose, he's achieved that (Jap designs I find tend to look good on the Japanese, but don't somehow manage to look the same on western shapes!).'

FRED

Fred lives in Brixton with Mum and Dad, 'but I'm never there. I'm usually out and about being promiscuous'. He works in Sprint, Covent Garden, and 'performs' Tarzan Grams about three times a week on unsuspecting victims in clubs and restaurants around the West End. Spends his spare time listening to Donny Hathaway, Jeffrey Osbourne and Aretha and goes to Do Do's at Busby's in Charing Cross Road every other Tuesday.

'I like the people, pick up a lot of fashion influences, drink whisky and orange till I fall over. Everybody seems to be out of their boxes, the music, (a mix of classic '70s disco sounds), is always good to dance to though there's not enough J.B.. The atmosphere's nice and tight, loads of lovely women and interesting guys. I'm amazed how some men can dress up and look so beautiful. I go to most places around town, the Wag, Mud, (Friday nights at Busbys), Warehouse and the Metropolitan used to be O.K.'

Wears: 'Contrasts, different from day to day. One day I'll be in '50s and leathers, the next I'll be in outsized suits from Sprint, (with discount), hats from Big Apple in Brixton, anything that suits me, trilbys, flat caps, leather skull caps and I go for silk scarves sticking out of pockets. Issey Miyake and Wendy Dagworthy stuff is on the case and anything from the roots of flower power, '67 was a good year for fab gear.

'I look around me these days and it depresses me a bit, yobs who used to take the piss out of people for wearing diamanté and patent shoes are getting into it themselves now it's become easily available and High street, they don't know shit you know, all this electro crap they think they're the pinnacle of the soul scene, they must've been into something else, they don't appreciate the origin of the sounds man, the real dances, it's a shame. I blame it on the Government, I mean they say all good things come round again but we still got a few years of Thatcher and that yet.

MASH!. DIG! KILLER! i-D STYLE! Take a brogue, a cravat, a key-chain or a weejun — mix it up with a backless cape coat, a button-down trenchcoat, a wispy peach suede double-breasted waist-coat; a silky white Brooks Brothers shirt and double-fly boxer shorts — top it off with a red velvet Texan tie and silver tongued patter, a bit of blag, a bronze fedora...and BOB'S YOUR UNCLE!

Instant style! – a modern day anachronism that strays from the shop floor and marches into the real world of street fashion, and waltzes back again into the chintz and glints of marbled dancefloors! Let fashion live! Professional eclecticism? You bet! In the '80s the revolts into style and the plunder-blunders have been rife, ripe and fruity – turning Britain, and in particular London into a living, breathing catwalk of style. Where *every* living person is a new dress code – hundreds of thousands of new cults being born every ten minutes – each style turning into a faded snapshot, a framed snapshot.

And in these eclectic '80s, *i-D* has undertaken to be the gallery for all these snapshots – a rogues gallery, a beauty gallery . . . THE GALLERY OF STYLE. In this fashion exhibition the magazine has included everyone from Boy George to Lady Di, Jeffrey Hinton to Eric Stanton, from Tasty Tim to Cerith Wyn Evans, Anne Pigalle to Madonna . . . from the doors of the Wag Club to the wastelands of the Cairngorms. So – take a dip into the big bad world of cultural hybrids and idiosyncratic mish-mash: 1,000,000 people with twice as many ideas . . .

i-D magazine – conceived, edited and published by former *Vogue* Art Director Terry Jones hit the London news stands five years ago, in August 1980 – an A4 landscape size staple-bound issue of forty pages containing straight-up photographs of some of the most original looking and original dressing people in town. These pictures weren't created in an expensive fashion studio – they were either taken on the street or in front of some rapidly erected backdrop in someone's front room: REAL FASHION, REAL PEOPLE . . . identified for all to see. Nearly thirty issues later and *i-D* has photographed thousands of people, broadening out into what has become known as 'The Worldwide Manual Of Style' – the indispensable document of fashion, style and ideas. *i-D* was quarterly for three years, a bible of what to do and where to go – showing all kinds of fashion in every avenue and alley-way of style.

Scores of photographers, journalists, designers and stylists have passed through the hectic offices of *i-D*, all of them contributing in some way to the spark of the magazine. But it is a close-knit

FIVE YEAR FASHION FURY

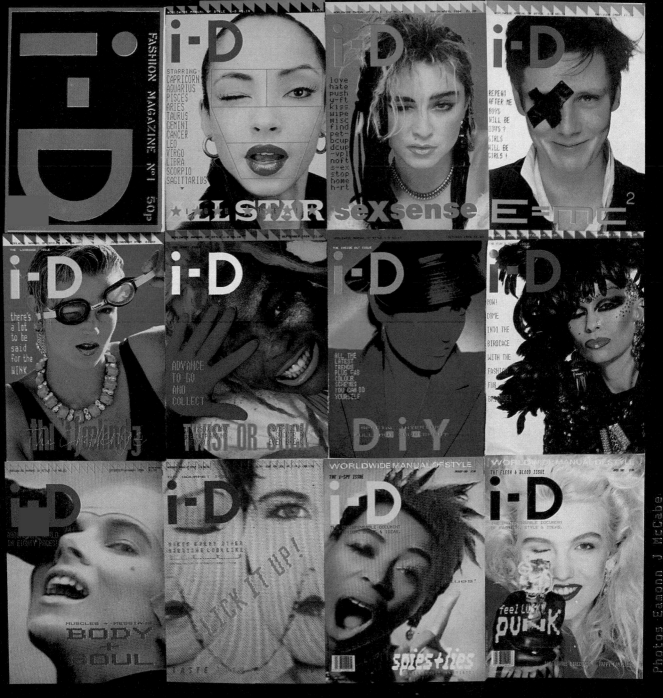

"Most magazines invite you to sip and chew; i-D
encourages you to swallow" - Caryn Franklin,
Fashion Editor

crew (the *i-D* wrecking crew) who forge together in a team effort to bring you the best, and to bring it *first*! *i-D* is a crusade that people want to get involved in – a crusade of style that envelopes *everybody's* past, from punk-hippy-art school-soul-smooth etc . . .

After the brief financial collaboration with Fiorucci, in Jan '84 *i-D* changed the format of the magazine, and went upright. The first portrait issue had Sade on the cover, more colour, more accessible layouts and *more* news.

The next step for *i-D* was in the autumn of last year when Terry Jones joined forces with *Time Out* publisher Tony Elliott, and with this business support, the magazine went monthly. The *i-D* crew also moved from the one room loft in Sherriff Road to the new premises in Covent Garden. But what *i-D* retained through all these changes was a passion and knowledge of fashion journalism that remains unsurpassed. *i-D* picks the cream of the world's fashion designers and pop stars way before anyone else. The industry were the first people to catch on to the game, picking up on *i-D's* ideas, recycling them and feeding them out to the mainstream. But the magazine remains the most influential handbook currently publishing, and with the increased legibility, and

more accessible layouts, *i-D* are still forging ahead with a vengeance.

i-D has not been one to ignore its readers and is ready to take the criticism with the applause. The complaints department on issue No. 1 logged 'Bloody fingers from staples', and the remarks over the past sixty months have included 'Impossible to read', 'Too pretentious' and even 'More erotic shitting'. They listened to them all.

Every issue of *i-D* is a historical document of the moment, the first issue now worth £20; every issue up to No. 9 being sold out (one of the most popular being No. 3, which had The Scars gold flexi-disc). So – in the past year, *i-D* has continued to mirror the backwaters and catwalks of London's streets – taking in the world of paupers and pop-stars. Not only have *i-D* been scouring the nation's capital for the best dressed chickens in town, but they have also been going further afield to find the source of innovative fashion – Birmingham, Hull, Liverpool, Bristol, Newcastle, Dublin, New York, Tokyo, Los Angeles, Milan, Paris . . . nowhere is too far for the *i-D* tribal bible cameras to travel.

'*i-D* is the only magazine that goes out to meet its readers, asks them what they think and finds out what they're doing' – Alix Sharkey, *i-D* contributor.

"i-D brings the street into the studio and takes the studio into the street" - Dylan Jones, Assistant Editor

A recent innovation has been the *i-D* Yellow Pages: an exhaustive list of where to buy clothes of allsorts, in and out of London. From Katharine Hamnett outlets to porno-butch cock-ring stockists. Each issue has its own particular theme – be it sex, money, flesh and blood, religion, food, interiors or red hot – allowing *i-D* journalists to rack their brains and fathom facts from every part of the encyclopedia. In the last twelve months the magazine has included interviews with Peter York, Richard Ingrams, Ken Livingstone, Run DMC, Al Matthews, Paul Morley, Stephen Bayley, Takeo Kikuchi, Jean Paul Gaultier, Ken Campbell, Fay Weldon, Julien Temple, Dianne Brill, Neil Spencer, Anne Pigalle, John Maybury, Andrew Logan, Eric Stanton, Lord Kennett to name a few . . . talking to the brains behind the faces. The premise behind the magazine has always been that EVERYONE has a chance – and in 1984 *i-D* continued the i-Dea by presenting the best of the young designers, clubbers, singers, bodypoppers, motorists, bouncers etc . . . *i-D* broke the mould by presenting John Richmond and Maria Cornejo with their classic v-necks with back-long zips; John Galliano's Afghanistan Repudiates before he hit the big-lig-time with American buyers a-go-go; Alice Rycroft's Captain Scarlett style for Atom; the gladiatorial Pam Hogg colour explosion . . . and '84 also heralded patent leather; bras on the outside and bras on the inside with nothing on the outside; tartan and paisley paving the way . . . brocades, golds, flowers, petals and the great Crolla blanket-plunder: at the Spring '85 collections at Olympia there were more brocade waistcoats and more floral trews than you could shake a stick at: BRIGHT!

Up, up and away we went with long shirt tails; satin & tat; bleached bobs and white lips – the band 8th Wonder epitomising the '60s re-tread – bright, bouncy, mini-skirted and high thighed! Glitterati, platforms and pop-socks went overboard with the whine and dine; John Crancher with his silky doggeral; spots, disease and infectious infection by Spend Spend Spend courtesy of Leigh Bowery and Rachel Auburn; the blazen blazered cheek of Bazooka . . . and Bernstock and Spiers and BodyMap re-affirming their international status.

Katharine Hamnett's chic-guerilla look (a navy army resplendent in linen and silk baggy togs) – socially acceptable and anti-social utility work-wear . . . revolting into style. Plus of course the slogan t-shirts, started by Hamnett and

"i-D is the only magazine that goes out to meet its readers, asks them what they think and finds out what they're doing" - Alix Sharkey, i-D contributor

copied by Wham!, ZTT and everyone from pop-papers to DJs doing a spot of on-the-spot self-promotion. Men in skirts came back in a *big* way: towels, shawls, kilts, Richmonds and African prints – not many men wore them, but those that did looked brilliant. Then there were the Paul Smith t-shirts (black, pale blue and pink) worn with a pair of sailor's bags or Levis white tag workwear jeans – casuality in the extreme. And talking of casuals, Saturday night beneath the plastic palm-trees came to fruition in the form of Disco-pubs across the capital and the designer-conscious exhausting themselves by searching for the most expensive clothes available. Jewellery leapt with a vengeance – gold chains around polo-necks, medals and sparkles, plastic rings, braces, badges and smiley patches, Epitaph jewellery covering bods – the idea was ACCESSORIZE!

As the staff in the Yohji Yamamoto South Molton Street shop cut their fringes to forty-five degrees, as tattered red-tag Levis over tailored suits flourished in Holland Park, as square-toed boots – painted eyelashes and Tom Binns fish jewellery paraded down St. Christophers Place . . . the American buyers came out of the closet and swamped the designer collections. 1984 was the year that the pound fell and the designers flourished. And if you weren't anything else . . . you were and wore white spikey hair and shaved heads for girls . . . and flat tops and buffalo boys were tops. YOW!

'i-D hasn't yet fulfilled its potential as an all-encompassing fashion magazine . . . most magazines invite you to sip and chew, i-D encourages you to swallow.' – Caryn Franklin, Fashion Editor.

Today, the glossy magazines are catching up a lot quicker than they did five years ago, keeping i-D on its toes with its ear to the ground and its heartbeat on the street. And even though fashion designers are now stars before they leave college, first year fashion students get spreads in Italian fashion magazines, buzz-words in razz-mags . . . i-D keeps on the case. Fashion designers might be the new artists of the 20th Century, having sparse shops with empty rails and half a dozen garments on sale (the haute couture for the elite being the equivalent of buying paintings), but the i-D gallery is the *true* shopfront of style . . . opening the doors and raising the curtains. i-D makes your day.

'i-D brings the street into the studio and takes the studio into the street' – Dylan Jones, Assistant Editor.

"I'll go along with that" - Terry Jones, Editor

I AM FIVE FEET TEN INCHES

Have blonde hair, blue eyes – and would like to be a model

TROJAN

MODELS OF THE YEAR?
Who would ever have guessed.

A collection of more unlikely looking 'models' one could not have imagined . . . The dictionary describes a model so:

'an object of imitation; exemplary; excellent of its kind.'

This was a year which threw up ALL kinds. A girl that looks like a boy; a girl that looks like nothing on earth; a sex-change; a Buffalo; AND Suzy Bic!

Oh my, oh my, what would Lucy Clayton have made of all this? Where is the poise? What is the pose? How many of them look as though they could read a book, let alone balance one on top of their heads??? Where is the charm in this new school? Quite simply in its diversity, and awareness of personal beauty. Their charm being that none of them are perfect. Far from it. They could be you, they could be me. They are further re-affirmation of that old adage that it's not what you've got, but what you do with it that's important. Why hide that stick insect neck – stick it out and sell it. This motley crew of models are characters, as opposed to being grotesque caricatures of beauty.

In this fantastic world of fashion here are these REAL people staring out at us from the pages of glossy magazines . . . and that's what makes them so appealing, and why we like to see them as often as possible, and it's that which has earned them the title of 'Models of the Year'.

Here we see them through the eyes of another.

Artist, Trojan has spent a large part of the year on the catwalks, and in front of the cameras, in New York, London, and Tokyo. He was heralded by respected fashion writer Sally Brampton in the OBSERVER as the possible 'Face of '84' . . .

Some year, eh?

THESE ARE MY IMPRESSIONS OF THE MODELS OF THE YEAR... TROJAN.ᴥX

GOING TRANSATLANTIC WITH
TERI TOYE.

Q. How did you become a model?
A. I met someone who asked if I wanted to become a model – I didn't really, but then Sprouse started doing his thing and he asked me, and I did. Then other people wanted me to model for them . . .

Q. Have you always been interested in fashion?
A. Yes I have, and I studied fashion design at Parsons.

Q. Do you have a favourite model?
A. Yes I do.

Q. Who do you like?
A. Laurence Treil.

Q. Whose clothes do you like wearing?
A. I like to wear clothes in Paris . . . I also think the clothes in London are good too, but I've never done any shows there . . . but here in New York nothing's really happening . . . it's very dull.

Q. Do you think you'll always be a model?
A. Oh God, I hope not . . .

Q. Following on from that do you believe in Andy Warhol's fifteen minutes of fame? Is yours over or has it just begun?
A. Well I guess there's something in it. It certainly worked for Andy, and he's gotten a long fifteen minutes.

Q. Have you styled yourself on anyone?
A. Not really, it just happened.

Q. What do you feel about all the girls who have copied your look?
A. I don't care that they do it . . . that's THEIR problem.

Q. How do you feel when people talk about you as model of the year?
A. Well, I've just been through all that in New York where they chose me as the face of the year . . .

Q. And how did that feel?
A. Well, I don't know . . . it doesn't really change anything, it's just that somebody decides something . . . it doesn't really mean anything. We'll just have to see what happens . . .

Q. Has changing your sex been valuable to your career as a model?
A. I've never changed anything . . .

Q. What size are your feet?
A. What size are my feet?

Q. Yeah . . .
A. Nine.

SUZI BIC
Height 5.8½ Bust 34
Waist 23 Hips 35
Dress Size 10 Shoes 5½
Inside Leg 33 Outside Leg 43
Hair Black Eyes Green

● Suzi Bic is represented by Premier

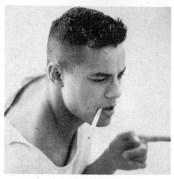

NICK CAMEN
Height 6.0 Suit Size 40R
Chest 40 Waist 30
Collar 16 Shoes 8
Inseam 33 Outside Leg 43
Hair Dark Brown Eyes Blue

● Nick Camen is represented by Laraine Ashton

AMA

AMANDA CAZALET
Height 5.11 Bust 35
Waist 25 Hips 35
Dress Size 12 Shoes 7
Hair Black Eyes Brown

● Amanda Cazalet is represented by Marco Rasala

TERI TOYE
Height 5.10 Bust 34
Waist 24 Hips 34
Dress Size 6/8 Shoes 9
Hair Blonde Eyes Blue

● Teri Toye is represented by Click

LESLIE WINER
Height 5.10 Bust 34
Waist 24 Hips 36
Dress Size 10 Shoes 7½
Hair Blonde Eyes Blue

● Leslie Winer is represented by Name

FACING UP TO '85

First comes powder factor number one, eyeliner, lip gloss oh it's all such fun

LYNNE EASTON She trained at Joan Price's, after leaving she started testing and worked freelance before joining her agency Creative Workforce. She enjoys fashion work best but mostly works for the music business. Groups she has made-up include Culture Club, Wham!, The Style Council and Spandau Ballet.

SALLY FRANCOMB Hair. Sally Francomb, at Vincent Lonro for Premier, came to London two years ago with one suitcase. She had always wanted to be a hairdresser, liking the 'transformations' which hairdressing allows her. She decided to go freelance because 'it is so creative, and you get round the world . . . travel, which I enjoy'. Eventually she hopes to get into films. Whose hair would she most like to style? 'Sam Shepperd'. Why? 'Because he's dishy . . . he hasn't got much to do . . . but I'd like to run my fingers through it!'

THE LOOK Combines later '60s style with an Indian influence which was very strong earlier this year.

Model: Sherry at Premier, **Styling:** Lorraine Kinman, **Clothes:** Pam Hogg, **Jewellery:** Necklaces; Susan Wainwright at Liberty Earrings, Broaches and Rings; Dinny Hall at Liberty, **Photo:** Peter Brown

LOUISE CONSTAD Worked in magazines where she learnt about make-up. In 1982 she joined Laraine Ashton. Has worked with Norman Parkinson, Terence Donovan, Lord Snowdon, Clive Arrowsmith for VOGUE, HARPERS & QUEEN, TATLER. Has made-up Faye Dunaway, Alison Moyet, Angela Rippon, Selina Scott, Depeche Mode and Adam Ant.

STEPHEN HAMILTON Trained as a Social Worker and never dreamt of becoming a hairdresser. He began styling hair of Lady Sloanes and ambassadors' wives. He heard that Cuts salon was 'in the groove' and looking for an energetic stylist. He has worked with them for the last two and a half years. He has done hair for Glen Matlock (Sex Pistols), Morrissey (Smiths), John Moss (Culture Club). He feels the future should be full of glamorous party styles to cheer everyone up.

THE LOOK A picture with feeling and story: The London Tourist. An attempt to show the changes in London in '85 e.g. the discontinuation of the £1.00 note and taking Eros to the cleaner. We used all things immediately identifiable with London. The slogans are back. I'm backing Britain.

Model: Anna Curtis at Models One, **Styling:** Rachel Williams, **Clothes:** London print shirt and jacket by Mark & Syrie, **Jewellery:** Prism at Hyper-Hyper, **Hat:** Carnaby Street, **Photo:** Peter Brown

KAY MONTANA Kay knew what she wanted to do while at school. When she left at 16 she met photographer Jamie Morgan and started testing. She worked with Jamie for the FACE in January 1984 and since then has gone on to work for magazines such as LEI, JILL, ITALIAN VOGUE, HARPERS & QUEEN. She works mostly editorial.
SALLY FRANCOMB Hair.

THE LOOK Lolita, Chiquita. In an age of lost innocence, all innocence is lost.

92   Model: Charlotte at Premier, Photo: Eamon McCabe, Styling: Sarah Edwards, Clothes: Flip

CAROL LANGBRIDGE Graduated from a four year fashion course at
St. Martin's School of Art in 1980. Advertising and editorial: HARPERS & QUEEN, VOGUE,
DONNA, LINEA ITALIANA, COMPANY and HONEY.

JAMES LEBON Trained with VIDAL SASSOON. He set up his own late night salon in
Kensington Market called JAMES CUTS. He gave up because 'it got so tacky', and moved
into expansive premises in Kensington Church Street. A sideways step into music had
James promising to 'SEXTIFY YOU . . . Cuts – I'll cut your hair – cuts – I'm debonair', he sang.
James is cool – his work is HOT!

THE LOOK Make-up should be adapted to suit models face shape and style. Martine has a
naturally strong look so foundation is kept pale and matt; eyes simple but not defined with
eye-liner. Her eyebrows have been darkened and grow naturally straight but this shape has
been exaggerated to become the predominant feature. Mouth is subdued to balance
against the eyes.

Model: Martine at Marco Rasala, Jewellery: Tom Binns, Photo: Peter Brown

93

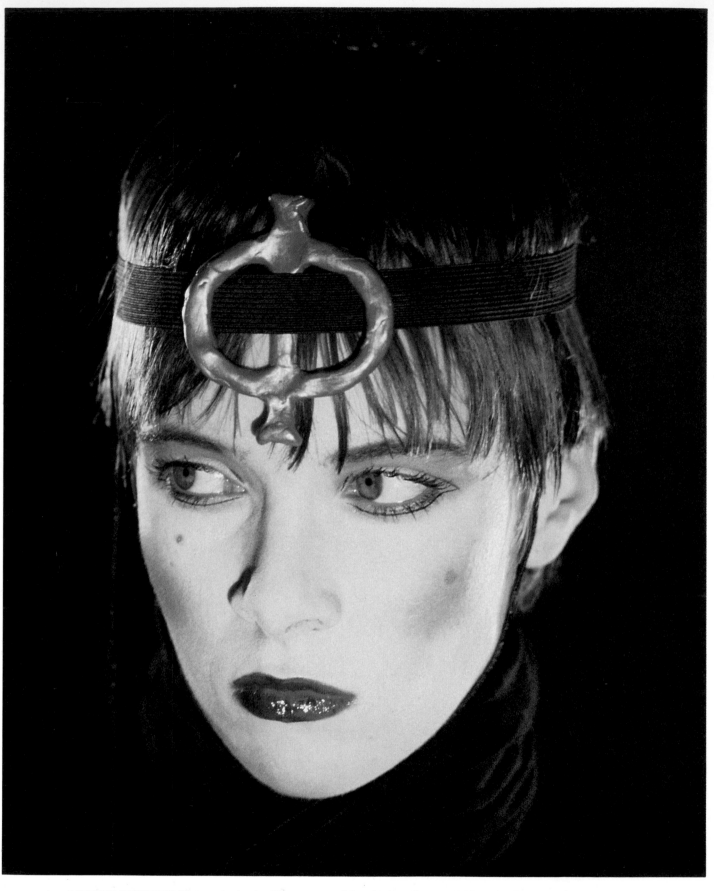

LESLEY CHILKES Three and a half years working in London and New York as make-up artist. Advertising campaigns and editorial for such magazines as VOGUE, HARPERS & QUEEN, TATLER, FACE, OVER 21, HONEY, AMERICAN VOGUE, MADEMOISELLE and Italian magazines such as LEI. Her star sign is Libra.

LAYLA D'ANGELO Hairdresser at Danielle Galvin colour salon. Has been working for ten years. London, Milan, New York. Editorial: HARPERS & QUEEN, OVER 21, FACE, i-D, LINEA ITALIANA. Her star sign is Capricorn.

THE LOOK Glossy, bright, whorish, messy, Fellini-esque, clogged, sexy, bitchy, sultry, uneven, scraped, childish, punkish, very tarty.

94

Model: Sandra at Z, Jewellery: Layla D'Angelo, Photo: Peter Brown

CHANGING SEX PAINLESSLY

A year when young ladies suited themselves

LAURA HARDY

In France they called it Le Style Bowie, in America they cited Annie Lennox and in England, Fleet Street labelled it Gender Bending. Whatever you choose to call it, this last year has seen a twist of all our rigid dress codes – the sexes have grown closer – men into skirts and girls into suits. We're cross dressed.

The fashion for women to raid their men's wardrobes is nothing new, but men borrowing from women has always been a little further back in the closet. Now out of the closet has come a riot of trailing lace, diamanté, wrapover skirts and diaphanous shirts . . . and not on the girls! Meanwhile the girls have been discovering the pleasures of sturdy lace-up shoes, razored crops, and the reassuring silhouette of a wide-shouldered jacket.

The seeds were sown in the minds of the masses by one clear image of inspiration. Last year the strong style of Annie Lennox stood out and stirred the imagination. With her tongue in cheek 'stubble' make-up and her immaculately tailored tartan suits she lit the fuse on a long line of mass market copies. She managed to transform herself so convincingly into a masculine style for the video of the Eurythmics major hit 'Who's That Girl?' that the American viewing public choked on their Big Mac 'n' Budweiser and demanded the banning of the video! 'Is it a chick?

Is it a guy? No . . . it's another weirdo, transvestite limey pop star.' Then, when the soothing fact that, she was indeed a she emerged, she was propelled into a household name and her style was *the* style. Ironically enough, those perfectly tailored suits were the work of the master crafter of the mass market, Jeff Banks. He has been both a catalyst and co-ordinator of the mannish suit for women. 'I first made men's suits for women in '75. That was when we really began adapting men's tailoring techniques to women's wear. Mark Tarbard, a brilliant cutter, who has worked with me on and off since then, did some big dog-toothed jackets for the Knightsbridge shop in '82. Annie Lennox saw them and we began making clothes for her. She has very strong ideas of how she wants to look. For winter '84 we put suits, not unlike hers into the Warehouse shops and they just roared out.'

Indeed they did, and they were the best. Though other chains attempted to produce wide-shouldered narrow-hipped jackets and baggy trousers, not one had a style to compete.

The mass market capitilised on male style, whilst men's wear

became perceptibly more exotic. The windows of men's chain-stores were suddenly a blaze of multicoloured pattern, bright blouson jackets, loud checks and showy accessories. Gee 2 (that most solid chain of acceptable men's wear) even went so far as to stock huge diamanté brooches, yes brooches, for the boys to pin on their lively blazers and transparent oversized shirts. Reports are they're selling like hot cakes . . . even in Scunthorpe.

The girls too needed the perfect details to suit their suits. The head to toe style was set with flat patent shoes. From traditional men's cobblers to the massive conveyor belts of high street availability went the modest patent leather lace-up. Where this vogue began is hard to say . . . it may have been Ray Petri's styling for the *Face* or it may have been an incredible collision of like minds but whatever it was, the patent shoe was the longest running success of '84/'85.

This last year has seen all manner of masculine style come into play. The skinhead girl of Carnaby alleyways and Northern estates looked suddenly so chic. Her heavy Doc Martin soles, her ill fitting Crombie, that aggressive

● All pictures by Kim Nott for *Harpers & Queen*

Harrington jacket all inherently English styles. Bernstock & Spiers, hyper-talented accessory designers, this year showed their first ever collection of clothes. 'the Yobbo Collection', a range of delightfully witty androgynous clothing complete with reversible check Harringtons, fringed jackets, wide-check cotton trousers, and their own trademark – a Yobbo badge. They succeeded in taking the skinhead girl's style and translating it into a palatable high fashion version. Another duo, Richmond Cornejo didn't let gender get in the way either . . . they took Prince's transvestite pop style and gave it back to the girls, with ankle length shocking pink duster coats and satin leggings.

● Boys flirt with sumptuous pastels. Photo by: Niall McInerney

Established designers, Betty Jackson and Wendy Dagworthy also created soft feminine mannish suits. Betty Jackson took the three button 'Mod' suit shape and made a neat flecked linen version of it, in pale blue and pale pink; little boys and little girls colours for both. Wendy Dagworthy meanwhile used the same exquisite linen and cut a far larger silhouette. Her jackets were for both men and women – the only barely discernible difference being the sizing. Her bold floral shirts were based on men's traditional stuffed shirts shape, with an inset panel of quiet liberty print thereby taking feminine fabrics, men's tailoring and creating a shirt for both sexes.

True merging and blending of the sexual borders.

On the catwalks during all the designer shows gender criss-crossed and crossed back, until the terms male and female were virtually redundant. Nowhere more so, than during the BodyMap show. Girlish boys wore women's clothes and boyish women wore men's

● Bernstock-Speirs had tatoos on you in '85

● Photo by: Niall McInerney

wear. BodyMap's startlingly bleak vision of a sexless, spaced out future, disturbed some, perturbed others, and delighted a few. Whatever reaction it provoked it was in many ways the most extreme and most revealing example of just how many rules have been crushed in the last year. Beneath the showy shock value of their controversial

styling they were giving us all food for thought.

Whilst the designers broke the rules on the catwalk, magazines photographed models with short hair and harsh make-up. The catalogues of Commes de Garçon, photographed by Peter Lindbergh captured a mood – increasingly severe but hauntingly beautiful – which in turn influenced fashion victims and boyish British Belles. Sophie Hicks of *Tatler* (long an exponent of androgynous beauty) fed us the same imagery, adolescent, innocent, and sexless. Her fashion features over the year set into motion a copycat craze of pudding basin fringes, and easy clothes. Ms. Hicks managed to pour the extremely female form of

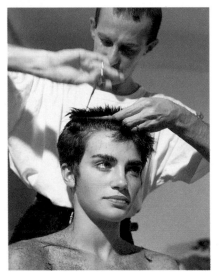

● A year when girls' hair reached the floor

Isabella Rossellini into raunchy leggings, black vests and leathers and an altogether cliché'd form of 'rock' style came alive in an unlikely reincarnation. So, from hard rock postures to little boy/girl lost, the girls stared out – in the glossy pages of *Vogue, Harpers* and *Tatler* and on the shiny images of tarty ads girls were boys.

The short haircuts cropping up everywhere owed much to the innovative New York and Paris hairdressers, to the original street looks of England and to a handful of talented cutters in London. One such, is Rene Gelston, ex-art director of Vidal Sassoon and now freelance, with published work in the Italian *Vogue, Linea,* the *Face*

● Never further from the terraces. Crombie girls battled
it out on the catwalks. Photo by: Martin Brading for
Company Magazine

ERRATA – THE FASHION YEAR VOL. III

The publishers apologise for the incorrect captions on pages 127 and 128.
The picture credits should be as follows:
Page 127 – Wendy Dagworthy Autumn/Winter '85.
Page 128 – First column – Chelsea Girl Autumn/Winter '83.
Second column – first photograph: Katharine Hamnett Autumn/Winter '85.
And apologies to Lynne Franks in whose chapter the errors occurred.

to name but a few. Rene set to the heads of any willing girl and experimented with clippers and razors until he perfected a technique that stands out amongst stylists.

'I developed a way of working using both clippers and scissors so that I could work fast. I always wanted to shed the hair fast so that I could see a style developing. Early on I was inspired by sailors' crew cuts and some of the radical London kids, I sat any girl who came in down and if she had good bone structure and strong eyes I'd talk to her and see if she could carry off a strong short crop. I'd go as short as possible without being

brutal. Models were difficult, they and their agents were frightened of going too short, but eventually some did. Anna Curtis was one of the first to really go for it.'

The *Sunday Times* even wrote about her crop, it was so new at that time. Since then, many girls have gone for short hair and found themselves much in demand.

Models with boyish faces and lean cheeks – etched with character – were the new stars. Lesley Winner, who has always been a model boy, reappeared, thinner than ever, blonder than ever. She did a Warehouse catalogue, a *Company* cover, a few pages in *Tatler*, the BodyMap show, then she disappeared again but shorn blonde

scalps remained. Actress Ann Carlisle, from cult film *Liquid Sky* where she played both male lead and female lead, posed for *Vanity Fair* in utterly androgynous clothes. It was hard to tell what she was, but whatever she was her style was compulsive. At the same time in New York a new model 'girl'

appeared; Teri Toy, who was definitely not all woman. 'She' shook the foundations of the New York agencies as the magazines fell over themselves to use 'her'. The long rangy body and dead straight 'wig' hair began another trend. Black polo necks and ski pants, Teri's look, show everything and nothing

– an androgynous costume that leaves nothing to the imagination.

Whenever fashion has shock value, its true meaning gets lost amongst sensationalism. They either moralise and load an innocent fad with earth shattering meaning or they pronounce any startling trend as merely a juvenile craze, of little consequence. In the past, cross dressing has been blamed for the corrosion of moral values, breakdown of sexual barriers and gradual decline of civilization as we know it. This last year something far more important happened. We have seen the beginning of a true relaxation of the clothing boundaries, for men

and for women. Petty outrage has given way to mild tolerance. Boy George in his own chaotically irreverent way has opened the door for ordinary mortals with a penchant for dressing up. Clothes after all, are fun. He has diffused the aggression which has always followed the eccentric and deflated the seriousness of trendsetting.

Fashion will always be a matter of life and death for some, entertainment for armchair voyeurs, and most importantly a very visible barometer of social change. Anthropologists take note 1985 saw men in skirts and girls in suits.

● Kim Nott for *Harpers & Queen*

● Film-maker Holly Warburton's study of model/sometime D.J./sometime personality Julia Fodor

MAPPING THE FUTURE

Talking 'bout my generation

STEVIE STEWART

 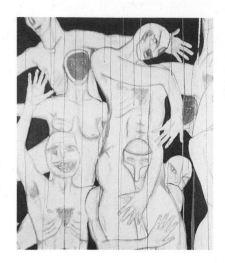 

There is a new generation emerging throughout England today, particularly from London which is now looked upon by the rest of the world as a focal point of creative energy in fashion, film, video, music and dance.

Some people are comparing this creative revolution to the '60s but in strong contrast to the '60s people today are more concrete in their attitudes and financial positions.

A new school of thought is developing. Commerciality, creativity, dedication, hard work and fun co-exist. Brave and courageous ideas which pour out of Britain, combined with sheer dedication and perseverance are now turned into commercial ventures.

One moves in ever-increasing circles of talented creative people who together provide a very strong force. Unlike other countries everyone in Britain is very supportive of each other: fashion designers, video and film makers, models, illustrators, dancers, journalists, make-up artists, pop stars and musicians interact. Versatility plays an important part in this youthful force, one does not necessarily have to be trained in a particular category, but, of course, there has to be drive, determination, confidence and self-motivation.

In this country we are very lucky in the fact that creative talent is quickly noticed and picked up. The press are always looking for something new but at the same time are still supportive of the more established set. The magazines such as *i-D, Blitz* and *Face* act as vehicles to show talent and – exactly what is happening in London not only in fashion, but also in related fields. These magazines are respected all over the world and treated like the bible especially in New York and Italy. Again contributors come from all walks of life and have their fingers in many pies. Although there is healthy competition there is no outright rivalry. This new generation joins forces to push through and break down barriers. A good example of this was last November when Brenda Polan, Fashion Editor of *The Guardian*, chose three fashion designers for the Dress of The Year Exhibition at Bath Costume Museum.

This new generation, once seen as a sleazy London set is now looked upon as an important force of the future. In London, social life, nightclubs and music are an important factor and humour is combined with hard work. London has always been a city where the youth and youth cults are part of everyday life. People refocused their attentions on London during the days of Punk which created the energy force that is now being channelled into a new do-it-yourself generation.

People doing-it-themselves often have to subsidise their businesses with other ventures, frequently in the form of market stalls or opening up nightclubs. For example, White Trash is run by one half of Bernstock and Speirs – Paul, accessory and clothes designer, and Dencil Williams; Taboo is run by Leigh Bowery, Fashion Designer; Wag Club's Total Fashion Victim is run by John Maybury, film maker and artist, Stephen Linard, fashion designer and Julia Fodor, model.

These clubs form meeting points and a lot of the successful people meet up to share some fun after a hard day's work, this being another important link in the circles. Music is provided by people like Jeffrey Hinton, famous for his disco-mixes, and who has also worked on many fashion shows. One can listen to the music of friends, some of whom have soared up the hit parade for example Boy George, Marilyn, Helen Terry, ABC, Haysi Fantayzee. Music plays an important part in fashion, interacting in the form of dressing, video, image and fans. Bands are now very aware of how they dress and how they present their public image. Fashion designers are dressing bands a lot more nowadays. It all helps to get the message across.

● The eyes of the new generation, David LaChappelle's half-cocked view of life

● Lesley Chilkes makes up the eyes of the new generation

Fashion is the message and the messenger, as Katharine Hamnett illustrates with her t-shirts, is a much more politically and sociologically aware youth. In some ways ecology and peace are becoming fashionable; pop concerts for miners, Band Aid etc. Jeremy, ex-Haysi Fantayzee, is an example of someone who has pushed his creativity through to commercialism. As well as enjoying the success of Haysi Fantayzee, Jeremy is also known for his Circus nightclubs, the roving party, and is now working on television adverts creating soundtracks for commercials such as Levis, British Airways, British Sugar and Pepsi. He will soon be moving into film soundtracks and a new direction in pop music.

John Maybury, film maker and artist, who found the name BodyMap, has had exhibitions and shown his films at the I.C.A. and the Tate Gallery. He also makes fashion show videos to subsidise his art e.g. Katharine Hamnett, Wendy Dagworthy, Jasper Conran and BodyMap, and pop videos such as Everything But The Girl and Helen Terry. David Holah of BodyMap, Helen Terry, Michael Clarke, George and Marilyn have all appeared in his films, Helen Terry wearing BodyMap clothes throughout her video. John Maybury also used Barry Kamen, whose first catwalk show was BodyMap, in his videos, and he is now an up and coming illustrator. Other artists such as Peter Doig are using T-shirts for their canvasses and selling these to Joseph. The Cloth also have art exhibitions as

● Photo by: David LaChappelle

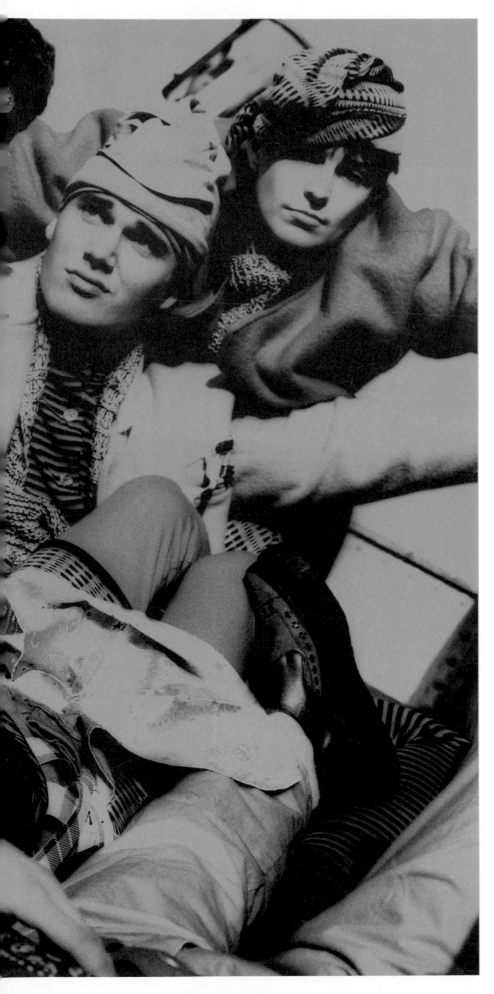

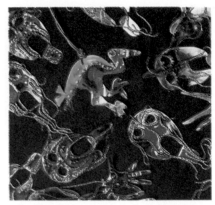

● Jewellery which screams at you by Corker and Curry

well as designing clothes and prints.

Michael Clarke, is another British success story, at twenty-two years of age he is one of Britain's brightest dancers and choreographers. He brings together some of the hottest talents in dance, rock and fashion in Britain today, by commissioning designers such as Leigh Bowery and BodyMap to produce costumes for his pieces. He uses Bruce Gilbert, formerly a member of influential band Wire, and the post-punk band The Fall and Jeffrey Hinton to provide the music and by using American film-maker/designer Charles Atlas, promotes the link with America. Since Michael, to date, has not used a set, the costumes and lighting are of great importance. He uses work by people that he admires, some of whom are his friends. Michael has recently commissioned Vivienne Westwood to design the costumes for his next piece. Here again dance, fashion, music and film are interconnected.

Connections with America are growing. There is now a lot of interaction between these countries particularly New York and London. It's a matter of working from the 'Inside Out' – whereas in the last decade, designers would, immediately after graduation, hop off to Paris, Milan and New York, people are now making a name for themselves in England and then commuting between England and America. BodyMap has signed a big American licence deal and continually commutes back and forth to New York to work on this project. John Galliano a recent

● Artist John Maybury and textile designer Hilde Smith as themselves

graduate from St. Martins was invited to go to New York but prefers to stay in London. Successful make-up artist Lesley Chilkes commutes to New York frequently. Layla D'Angelo creator of hair concepts works frequently in New York when she isn't starring in John Maybury's films or presenting BodyMap shows or designing and making jewellery.

Recently a young New Yorker has hit the London set, David La Chappelle, a talented photographer who has been used by BodyMap, *Vogue* and *Interview* magazine.

At BodyMap the circles move around, lots of creative people waft in and out. It is a young company employing other young people, mixing creativity with industry. Another important link working with David Holah and Stevie Stewart is Hilde Smith, trying to bridge the gap between fashion and textiles. She works alongside David and Stevie designing the BodyMap prints. Hilde also turns her hand to modelling and designs for Paul Smith and Liberty, Gloria Saks, Murjani, – Image Bank. Other examples of ex-Body-Mappers are; Janice Hall who then formed Memento with her boyfriend Bruno Broniecki and Corker and Curry (Alex Curry and Jen Corker) now jewellery designers.

With everyone turning their hands to different areas will the future bring a designer / artist / film star / pop singer / journalist / hairstylist / visagiste who all answer to the same name?

● Hilde Smith textile designer as model. Photo by: David LaChappelle

THE RAKE'S PROGRESS

As women make strides in liberation so too are men changing theirs . . . literally

THOM O'DWYER
STEPHEN KING

In the beginning there WAS fashion. Fashion for men, as well as for the fairer sex. Men have not ALWAYS been drably and drearily dressed. Historically, this is a very recent phenomenon. It has only in the last century-and-a-half, that man's dress has remained almost uniform in shape, colour and fabric.

The Bible tells us that the real reason for clothing was sexual modesty. Adam and Eve, when they realized their nakedness, 'sewed fig leaves together, and made themselves aprons.' However, there is absolutely no mention of Eve decorating her botanical mini-skirt with floral flounces and frills – historically, the first occurrence of unisex dressing!

From the Garden of Eden until the beginning of the nineteenth century, the line of division between male and female dress has been considerably blurred for the most part. To the modern eye, the most common difference or division is the skirt and trousers but virtually all the ancient civilizations – the Greeks, Romans, Cretans, Egyptians, the Etruscans, right back to Adam – all wore tunics or a similar type garment.

One factor that completely changed the face of men's attire was the development of tailoring in the fourteenth century. It was through the introduction of fitted and shaped clothing that the differentiation between male and female attire began to be truly felt. By this time most men had adopted a short tunic previously only worn by peasants and 'barbarians'. To this, since the legs were left exposed, was added the hose. The hose were attached to the short tunic or doublet and pulled tightly (since they were made from cloth cut to the shape of the leg, knitted stockings being not in common use until well into the sixteenth century) to get a smooth fit. Over this was added an upper garment. These three items – the doublet, hose and upper tunic – evolved into what is now the male suit of clothes. The proverbial three-piece suit.

For the last 300 years the main items that made up the male suit of clothes have both retained their instrinsic character and original names, aside from the change from knee-breeches and hose to trousers in the early nineteenth century. What was once doublet, hose and upper tunic now becomes coat or jacket, waistcoat and trousers.

In the vast history of costume male clothing has almost always been specifically designed to indicate and dramatise physical and social superiority or dominance. Through the use of strong colours, bulky material, and often times padding, the illusion of size and muscular strength was stressed.

Men's clothes have almost always been designed for active pursuits. Women's, on the other hand, have invariably been designed or concocted to promote physical frailty, immobility, subjugation. Interestingly, with the (very) odd exception, women's clothes have always been exclusively designed and made by men, not by their own sex.

It was the Industrial Revolution and the subsequent rise in power of the respectable bourgeoise that irrevocably changed the look, the form, function and decoration of men's clothing. Since this time political, sociological and moral views have persistently and pedantically ruled male clothing. Clothing rather than fashion – that is, until the 'Swinging Sixties', when the word 'Fashion' in men's wear returned.

From the middle part of the nineteenth century, it suddenly became 'ungentlemanly' to wear anything even remotely striking or vaguely conspicuous. Too great an attention to the latest styles of fashion or fastidiousness with personal appearances was forever after associated with frivolity, a typically feminine trait. A trait to be avoided at all costs by the sobre-minded businessman, the upstand-

● English Eccentrics. Photo by: Carrie Branovan,
courtesy of *Men's Wear*

ing pillar of society.

In a book on etiquette called *The Habits of Good Society* published in the 1840's (and cited by the eminent costume and fashion authority, James Laver, in his illustrious book *A Concise History of Costume*), the anonymous author outlines just what the well-dressed man needs to present a gentlemanly appearance. He recommends only dark blue or black for town wear, although he does allow a tweed suit for the country. Mr Laver pin-points this very period as the demise of men's fashion – fashion in the truest sense of the word – and the emergence of a sobre, sombre 'uniform' in heavier

● Anne Smith for Aditti. Photo by: Carrie Branovan courtesy of *Men's Wear*

fabrics, more subdued colours and restrained in cut. Urban camouflage. A disguise meant to enhance status by the very nature of its sameness. In 1897 *The Tailor and Cutter* proclaimed that, 'men, as a rule, are most conservative in dress. They adopt new styles very gradually, and, as a rule, care more for ease and comfort, practical utility and neatness, than for any new fashion that can be submitted to them.' Certainly it was a virtual impossibility to impose any revolutionary new fashion on men throughout the latter part of the nineteenth century.

Oscar Wilde and the whole Aesthetic movement was one fleet-

ing example of an attempt to shed the drab, tiresome trappings of bourgeois or middle-class respectability in male dress. It was short-lived and of little consequence.

Wilde's arrest and subsequent imprisonment for homosexuality cast a shadow over the whole Aesthetic movement, as well as the clothes he and his followers wore. Historically the incident may seem fairly superfluous and unimportant, however, in terms of the evolution of men's fashion, it had devastating effects. From the

● Jean Paul Gaultier. Photo by: Chris Moore

arrest of Oscar Wilde onwards any sort of flamboyance or eccentricity in dress was immediately and unequivocally labelled and categorised as effeminate, unmanly, and even subversive. Only homosexuals and deviants dressed in a manner that attracted attention. Real men stuck with their middle-class, urban camouflage in subdued and gloomy hues. This distorted attitude remained utterly fixed until the 1960s when many of the old prejudices gradually – with great reluctance – faded away.

In the 1960s rebellion and revolution were in the air. Youth Culture rocked and ruled the world. The concept of gentility which had kept men's clothes virtually static for 150 years was no longer accepted. 'We want the

world, and we want it now,' screamed a song by the popular group The Doors. In the 1960s, however, many of the sports clothes worn were completely classless.

The other prejudice, that only homosexuals wore flamboyant clothes, also began to disappear at this time. There was no doubt about the fact that the majority of the 'angry' young men who were wearing the latest Carnaby Street creations were distinctly masculine, 'Real Men'. The archetypal 'Butch Cockney' – epitomised by David Bailey and John Stephen, the generally recognised founding father of Mod fashion – made a conspicuous show of their 'bird

● Kenzo. Photo by: Chris Moore

watching'. At the same time, many of the 'dedicated followers of fashion' were truly 'gentlemen', by either descent or social background. One, Rupert Lycett Green, even opened a trendy London shop called Blades, which became the haunt for others, like Patrick Lichfield, from his class. The stage was set. The crusade to brighten men's clothes, classless clothes, had arrived. The break with tradition sparked the 'Peacock Revolution', liberating the wardrobes of men of all ages all over the world. In the 1960s, clothing-wise (and in so many other ways as well) men once and for all came out of their closets.

The 1970s – aside from a brief fashion fad called Glamrock, which was really the leftovers from the '60s – saw Punk appear in a wild burst of social protest. It was an overt and highly visual cry of rage coming from the marginally employed or unemployed working-class youth. Through outrageous shock tactics, the young Punks made people feel anger (if not outright rage), fear, guilt, compassion, revulsion – all simultaneously. This movement – fashion used to express political protest, urging political action – really was the birth of DIY Street Fashion. And this in turn has spawned a whole new generation of exciting

● John Galliano. Photo by: Johny Rozsa, courtesy of *Men's Wear*

young designers – many concentrating solely on men's wear, most at least dabbling in it – who have brought about in 1985 what the media has generally dubbed the 'New Peacock Revolution'.

Designer Tommy Nutter, a survivor of the '60s who was a top designer then as now, feels there is definitely an exciting new buzz in the air: 'There has been a big change in men's wear over the last two years. Punk and the whole street credibility thing have had a great influence. People are really interested in clothes once again. The difference between now and the '60s is that people are actually styling themselves up, rather than

being told what to wear and how to wear it. It is more of a romantic look happening now for men, and I feel that will definitely carry on. All the rich brocades, the fancy waistcoats, the jewellery. The most important thing that has happened is that the suit barrier has broken down, and men are finding their own individual style.'

Young men's wear designer, Dean Bright, is a total product of the '80s. Last summer at the St Martin's School of Art diploma show, he had the audience on its feet applauding his baroque collection of sumptuous purple velvets and satin. Since then he has set up his own business, designing clothes for top pop stars and for some of the chicest shops in London and New York. He has also shown his collection in both Tokyo and New

● Robert Budwig. Photo by: Francis Loney, courtesy of *Men's Wear*

York. Dean is extremely articulate when it comes to discussing the changing face of men's fashion in 1985: 'Men's wear is far more exciting than ever before. I would dare say it now leads fashion. In the direct sense, it has bypassed women's wear in terms of looking forward. So many women's wear designers are so derivative. It is, I feel, a natural progression from the late 1960s when women's wear designers were so prominent. I also think that a lot of it has to do with social conditions. Mass un-

employment in the UK has forced the kids to be far more creative and imaginative in putting together their outfits. I also definitely feel that London is almost solely responsible for this new explosion in men's fashion.'

On the subject of what he thinks is really so exciting, Dean says: 'Men are now playing around with clothes. Enjoying it, experimenting more. Unlike the '60s when the majority just bought the latest Carnaby Street creation that the Beatles or some other pop group was wearing, today the boys are having fun. I personally think of clothes like a toy. You play around and enjoy it.'

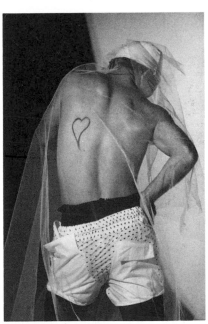

● Richard Torry. Photo by: Carrie Branovan, courtesy of *Men's Wear*

Certainly one major factor that has contributed to the 'New Peacock Revolution' was the formation two and a half years ago of the English Menswear Designer Collections (EMDC). The group has not only succeeded in stimulating the market and the industry but it has also made it far easier for young designers – like Dean Bright, John Galliano, John Crancher, and a host of others – to find acceptance.

Roger Dack, chairman of the EMDC, says: 'For us, 1985 really took off with a bang. All the big American buyers who have come over are raving about the men's wear, not so much the women's fashion. It used to be that all the art colleges tried to talk students out of specialising in men's wear. Some didn't even offer a course. Now it's different. They now see that a designer can make a very good living out of it, so it is now viable. The one thing that I personally feel is so exciting about men's wear is that there is no rule book any more. You can do what you want, mix up fabrics; different patterns, colours, experiment with new cuts or details. Almost anything, really. But at the same time, if you want to succeed, you have got to have the same design professionalism as a Levi's or a Mr Harry. Otherwise, forget it.'

● Crolla. Photo by: Carrie Branovan, courtesy of *Men's Wear*

Men's fashion in 1985 – and it *HAS* been a long time coming – is seemingly the media's proverbial flavour of the month. Virtually all the women's page fashion editors on the daily national newspapers – Suzy Menkes, Sally Brampton, Brenda Polan – all now dabble in men's wear (to a greater or lesser degree of success, and many women's magazines, like *Cosmopolitan* and *Options* now publish men's wear supplements. In fact, Suzy Menkes, fashion editor of *The Times*, said in an interview in *Men's Wear*, the trade's leading weekly magazine: 'In many ways I see no difference between men's and women's attitudes towards

clothes. The differences lie with the manufacturers and retails. In the past men's clothes tended to be dreary, and traditional firms refused to change. For some time now men's wear has been better value than women's.'

Whether this new-found (new-found since the 1960s, that is) interest is because of the sudden appearance of a whole new flock of exciting young designers like Dean Bright, John Galliano, BodyMap, John Crancher, the EMDC group, ad infinitum, or

● BodyMap. Photo by: Chris Moore

whether it is simply the appearance of a new generation of 'Bright Young Things' eager to throw off the dull brown, grey and navy dust cloths called suits, is difficult – no, impossible – to say.

Tom Gilbey, yet another star designer from the 1960s who has managed to bridge the gap and stay successful in the 1980s, is enthusiastic yet sceptical when discussing this 'New Peacock Revolution'. He emphatically states: 'It is definitely more exciting now, but at the end of the day I think it will level itself out. A lot of it is pure hype. Like in the '60s, it is all a big, huge orgasm. You peak and then you relax. You're all played out. What I think will happen is that it will level off, but still keep its momentum. Just not so extreme and so over-

exposed.'

So much of what is currently happening has to do with the breaking down of sexual stereotypes. Certainly (and we are still talking about a small minority, comparatively speaking) men are now less afraid to preen and be proud. As all the interviewees have said: 'In 1985, there are no rules.' For the first time in nearly two decades, a bit of excitement has returned to men's wear. In fact, you would be very safe in using the word fashion – men's fashion – forget the word clothing, or wear. That merely implies practical function. The men in 1985 want to be as pretty as the girls. Nothing to do

● John Galliano. Photo by: Chris Moore

with practicality really.

'Beauty at the moment,' says Tom Gilbey, 'is not my idea of beauty at all. It's ugly, decadent. In many cases, it is a grotesque look that is in. Certainly not my idea of beauty at all. But it *is* making a very important statement.'

Men's fashion *IS* making a very important statement, that is for sure. An orgasm? Yes, maybe. But the point is, an orgasm is fun. It is both a relief and pleasurable, albeit temporary. Let's just hope that this one – in 1985 – is a really big one! We men need it. Amen.

At last, men's wear comes of age. You no longer have to be a women's wear designer adding men's wear to your collections to get even the slightest recognition for the men's collection you have just completed. You can at last design men's fashion and acquire the acknowledgement from both the customer, press & media, that men's wear designers are just as talented, exciting, original and newsworthy (and in my view more so). Why now a change of events?

I believe it is because British men's wear designers are going out to counter the dominant women's wear biased of the press by attacking with a total front. Take the E.M.D.C. (English Menswear Designer Collections) for instance. Very few consumers have heard of this group of fifteen to twenty men's wear designers, predominantly English, but there is hardly a fashion media person who is not aware of its existence.

Two years ago, Roger Dack and myself decided enough was enough and formed the E.M.D.C. of which Roger is now Chairman. Too long had some great new and not so new talented creative men's wear designers gone unnoticed purely because they chose men's wear. Men's wear wasn't press-worthy for the Nationals, they wanted, as we say 'Tits and Bums' like, Miss Wigglebottom, and just how revealing can a dress become. Now the tide has turned. The established women are now look-

ing at the handsome man whose age is of no importance. Now it is more acceptable for younger men to escort and woo ladies who have for years looked after their appearance and bodies whilst the 'old man' bloats out on expense accounts and probably that pretty young filly from the office. The women are seeking and getting strikingly good looking men paying them attention, and the men love it. Now women phone the men to ask them out. So the man besides dressing to please and image create for himself has more reason to be aware of his body, hair, looks, health, clothes and style. That ridiculous feminist group who complain about anything that makes a woman feminine and look like a female have got their way.

Style being the appropriate word in this instant. Fashion has nothing to do with style. Fashion is 'in vogue' at that particular point in time, be it clothes, cars, where you live, jobs, one combination of life. Style is something we all want but not everyone can achieve.

Example

Anver – My assistant came to

my shop two and a half years ago, unemployed and unemployable, as a Junior/dogsbody. Now he has developed or should I say, been allowed to develop his own style which is much copied and has earned him great admiration from some of the most beautiful and sophisticated women I have ever seen. Even a National Institution like the *Sunday Times* recently interviewed him on how he got to where he is today. In a nutshell, he had 'style'. Clothes play a very important part in the style syndrome. You don't have to be rich to participate but it helps. You can put together a mode of dress which, to pinch a saying from you know who, 'says more about you than money can.' How true.

Over the past three to four years we have been offered uniforms to wear by the leading fashion houses. Men do not wear uniforms, unless they want to join the Forces or British Rail. They are and always will be independent of habitual tastes and style which vary only slightly from the main line.

Since the onslaught of the Black/Grey monotone clothes

● Hancher

● Donald Fong

● Hudson and Hudson

where very little of the wearers personality was allowed to overtake the 'total look' we have had time to reassess. What do we want from the clothes we wear? Comfort? Identity? Colour? Fun? or a combination, or none of these? Each one of these headings can be discussed at great length. My theory is going to be on personal experience from the contacts I have made over the past three years since the opening of the Kings Road shop. During that time I have learnt more about people and their style than in all my previous twelve years in the business. Before I opened the shop I, like a great many U.K. designers worked within a capsule, i.e. your contact was mainly with the buyer be it store or boutique buyer, for whom you relied upon for the money to enable you to carry on designing. A chicken and egg syndrome. I was never really free to do as I wanted. Now dealing primarily with the person who counts, the customer, I have been able to do as I have wanted and in time to give them what they desire to wear.

The monotone collections and overkill copies by the High Street stores of black provided a perfect springboard for *colour*. Jewel colours, rich and unashamed. The transition between black and colour was a very quick affair. When a person used to wear all black and would then put on a bright coloured shirt, the colour and black complemented one another adding zest and a new dimension to the clothes. Instead of being a flat two dimensional outfit the colour made it three dimensional. Buzzing of the hair changed the mood from 'throwaway chic' to a more definite decision to the clothes one wore. From the colour clash of Autumn/ Winter '84 to the new silk and Arabian fabrics for '85 in peacock and lamés, gold and metal, in rich three dimensional fabrics.

Man has arrived. He knows where he's at, clothes should not intimidate him, good clothes don't. Jean Paul Gaultier helped give status to the fabric story for men by being based in Paris. Journalists still believe that even if UK designers design it or are doing it, it needs a Paris name to give it the seal of approval. What the press don't realise is that we (Jones, Paul Smith, Scott Crolla and myself) have been selling it to the customers for at least two years, educating the customer, advising and experimenting. Giving flavour to a classic shirt by making it in two or more fabrics, or as in Charlie Allens case, suits and outer-wear, wonderful classic jackets and trousers in toning stripe, check, paisleys, very wearable and very subtle. Anthony Kwoks has given a different look to evening wear for men, silk voile jackets in see-through turquoise blue. His collections are always

● John Bellwood

taken to the extreme but always stunning and exciting. He is not afraid to experiment as to what or how far one can go with men's wear.

Last year the E.M.D.C. joined forces with Smirnoff to promote the new men's looks directly to the consumer. Thus overriding the boutique or store buyer and giving the consumer a chance to see what choice he would have if the buyers didn't dictate their own likes and dislikes so strongly when viewing the designer collections. The response was sensational to say the least, every night of the all round Britain tour it played (I use the word play because fashion shows are like theatre and should entertain as well as inform the viewer) to capacity crowd. As a result,

● Stephen King. Photo by: Francis Loney

● A.G.K. Potter

consumers were asking their local shops to stock certain items and designer labels and making the buyer aware of what the consumer wants i.e. a chance to be original, a choice of colour pattern and shapes. Invariably word gets out about a 'fashion tip' like paisley. 'Overkill' time is here again. Suddenly you get paisley knitwear, paisley ties, and paisley shirts, but even with overkill, colour is still coming forward, always allowing you to choose what suits you best.

Unlike women's wear designers

● Willi Wear

the majority of men's wear designers work within the confinements of what he or she feels a man will wear. More he than she, for unlike women's wear where there seems to be more men designing for women, men's wear is predominantly men designing for men, so without putting the point too bluntly, a man knows just how far he should go without ever being too restrictive. Although make-up, perfume, jewellery are all readily acceptable for men nowadays, skirts still have a long way to come and quite honestly can you imagine catching a No. 11 bus in the rain and hoisting up your skirt? Great idea for beach holidays as a variation on the sarong but not town wear. If I were to try one of I'd look like a cross

● Anne Smith for Aditti

between Yul Brynner and Shelley Winters! The mood today is relaxed, putting yourself and others around you at ease, yet still being able to stand out from the crowd without looking ridiculous or offending people. Gimmicky fashions are the good or bad, whichever way you tend to view it, method of trying to be fashionable. Like 'street fashion', much talked about and written about, it got to a point that everything was 'street' and nothing was really to do with clothes.

Clothes are the artist's pallet from which a person can choose what he is saying visually when he walks into a room or restaurant. Speaking of which the Brasseries have a lot to do with the new trend in clothing. Now you can actually

see the clothes, fit, colour and person who is wearing them and besides seeing the person you can actually talk to them, remember talking? Instead of standing on the edge of the Camden Palace balcony mean and moody in a shadow of an outfit, today you say 'hello' and laugh or moan as is your wish and discuss what the hell you want. Looking around the Dome, Criterion and Soho Brasseries etc. the standard of clothes on the guys are, I feel much better than a lot of the women's. They are strong, physical. You can actually see the shape of the person beneath the clothes. Unlike the shapeless monotone kimono of last year. At long last after two to three years of working out a guy can actually enhance all that effort by wearing clothes that show his torso and he can again use body language to communicate as he did before the androgynous period when boy/girl was the same outfit and we tried not to say if we were of either sex. An interesting period and a healthy one as we all got to know and understand our own sexuality and clothes are about as much to do with sexuality as one can get. Being a hunter by nature be it sexual or financial, clothes attract your prey or can warn your prey, like the medallion man hanging over the bar at the Hippodrome waiting for his 'dollybird' to appear. Every type of fashion has a role to play whether we like it or not.

It's nice to think that for the first time, men's wear designers are in such a strong position that even women are being influenced by our fabrics, colours and shapes. Was it not men's wear that started the brocade and eastern colours, the fez and chinese type suits? These were quickly picked up by some of the less reputable female department stores. England has always been a hot bed for talent, not only in men's wear and women's wear but in music and nowadays it's through music that men's wear is having its greatest impact. Every singer or group automatically makes videos and videos are seen by people and as (without hammering the point home too much) the music business is male dominant, so we get a variety of clothes being exposed to a group of fashion interested people who don't necessarily want to copy the artists but see the clothes being worn and styled properly. Today's pop videos are like mini fashion shows, – the Clash with their patent DM's or Paul Young with his jewel rich tweed suits, showing the customer that he too can wear a classic suit without having to buy a navy or grey pinstripe. Shirts too have been and still are a very big fashion feature in the men's wear. The long tails are very much an '85 phenomenon and are worn outside the trousers giving a relaxed and at ease feel to the wearer. Women too are picking up on the men's shirt trend, they are buying men's shirts for themselves. When

● Stephen King, Autumn '85

asked why they usually reply 'it's the fabric', or 'the fit' or both, they are speaking with their purchasing power and also because there is more choice in men's wear. Women's wear has become too mass marketed again, overkill on style, something which doesn't happen to the same extent in men's wear.

If we all looked like Nick Kamen, Matt Dillon or Prince Andrew and had the personality to go with it, we wouldn't need fashion, but 99.9% aren't the above and today, more than before, as technology advances and we become even more of a number we need fashion. You, the man, must stand out, feel strong of character and we the British designers are helping you to do that.

YOU ARE NOT WHAT YOU WEAR

Or how one t-shirt tried to change the world

JULIE BURCHILL

Photo courtesy of Rex Features

Photo courtesy of Associated Press

It is a popular, comforting, vainglorious modern myth that something so easily come by, so enthusiastically bought and sold as CLOTHES can be SUBVERSIVE, POLITICAL and even, on a good day, REVOLUTIONARY. Ever since the Jazz Age the rise and fall of the female hemline has been seen as the harbinger of some big freeze or say cheese breeze of change from the emancipation of women to the end of the world. There has emerged a whole philosophy of cut, cloth and social conscience – THE CHIC SHALL INHERIT THE EARTH.

The idea of shmutter cutter as an architect of social change stems from the monumentally confused sociologists of the '60s, who saw through austerity-coloured glasses – *they* had been teenagers in the fashion-rationed late '40s – the use of personal style as a means to the end of the political revolt. This is an old, odd notion still popular with certain frozen Western minds; the otherwise lucid Robert Elms can claim that, 'fashion is a much more important medium of change than politics', while Katharine Hamnett can actually claim that a designer can, 'come out with a look which changes the world for six months on a certain level'. *HEAVVVY.* These are what are known as delusions of grandeur; fashion may shock – I have been barred entrance to a dining car while wearing a GOD SAVE THE QUEEN T-shirt in 1977 – but it *never* subverts. The moral vanities of certain designers serve the narcissism of their clientele rather

than society as a whole.

Rebellious dressing is a substitute, not a spur, to political action. You won't see any Hamnett T-shirts at Greenham Common, even though she claims to have been inspired by them. The women of Greenham dress as though they have just come in from doing the gardening. Arthur Scargill dresses like a man set for a night out in a Northern wine bar, bald patch, Brut hairspray in the shiny vinyl manbag and all. Mrs Joan Ruddock dresses like a beautiful Marks & Spencer matron on her way to slave over a hot meals on wheels trolley. All of them dress like paragons of provincial, bargain basement respectability – and *all of them have their phones tapped* – the acid test of Governmental fear and loathing.

Couture castrates. The well-dressed will never take to the streets in armed insurrection – they'll be too scared of snagging their new clothes on the barricades. People who dress like Cavaliers will never behave like Round-heads. If you dress shockingly, you will never get the *chance* to subvert. The world is run by men in cheap,

dark, serviceable suits who can only be thwarted by men – be my witness, Philby, Bettany, Ponting – wise enough to adopt the un-impeachable protective colouring of respectability. The girl in the street in her expensive Katharine Hamnett DON'T DIE sandwich board does not cause Mrs Thatcher to lose a moment of sleep – sweet little Sarah Tisdall in her soft Benetton separates did, and went to prison because of it.

Fashion, like pop music, is a playpen, and those who devote a good deal of their time and energy to dressing up are about as frightening to the powers that be as someone repeatedly dressing and redressing a Christmas tree or papering and repapering his walls. Believe it. The way you dress is meaningless, and what's wrong with that; unless you're one of these people who is so insecure that you have an identity crisis every time the labels come loose in your clothes? It is as meaningless to the real meat and motion of life as the food you eat and the records you play, so what? It is a well-camouflaged puritan ethic that drives people to insist that clothes

GOD Save THE QUEEN

Sex PistOls

STAY ALIVE IN 85

SAVE THE WORLD

WORLNIDE NUCLEA BAN NOW

MEAN something, as macropsychotics and rockists used to do about their particular hobbies. But no food or music bore, however crazed, these days, claims that a perfectly-cooked *filet Mignon* or a Bruce Springsteen record stands a chance of changing the world. Clothes hobbyhorses still actually *say* this.

You are NOT what you wear, anymore than you are what you eat. Excessive fussiness about clothing, every bit as much as health food faddishness, indicates a small, frightened mind aware of the size, disorder and just plain *danger* of the world and neurotically desperate

● Kim Philby. Photo courtesy of Camera Press

to create *order* in a tiny part of it – even if it is only the mirror or the table. Of course it is nice to dress well – but it doesn't MATTER, and it is essentially something that the powerless find consolation in (women rather than men, young rather than old, Western Europe rather than Russia and America: satellites preen, but superpowers dress down). The powerful never really care about how they look, and neither do the people the powerful lose sleep over. But the puritan strain drives people to keep on droning on that clothes MEAN something; because to admit that it was all just KICKS –

like food and pop – would make the wearer seem unbearably shallow and hedonistic, fiddling with his cufflinks while home burns.

The sad paradox of all the '80s stylists is that their byline is the much-loathed sloppy '60s party-line in new clothing. Just change your hair, your clothes, your consciousness and the world changes with you; tune in and drop out has

● Greenham Common women. Photo by: Mark McKenzie.

become dress up and drop out. It is no coincidence that slogan T-shirts have become respectable for the first time since the '60s. This too is a decade of play-protest, where dressing for the revolution is an end in itself. DRESSING FOR THE APOCALYPSE – FASHION AS GUERILLA WARFARE, the Hamnett headlines primped in 1985, and designers are still talked

● Power dressing. Photo courtesy of Associated Press

of – incredibly – as 'taking risks'. Meanwhile Mrs Thatcher became the first ever British Prime Minister to host a cocktail party at Number Ten in honour of British fashion designers and their contributions to trade in 1985, while Norman Tebbit, her Ubermensch Dobermann, announced a new £20 million *grant* to help small firms in the textiles, clothing, knitting and

footwear industries. In China fashion is a major carrot in the shift to state capitalism. Of course excessive interest in clothes among the young ruled is a great help to the old rulers; youth aligning themselves by tribal fashion will fight each other, whereas youth without fashion organized along *class* lines will fight the powers that be.

Clothes are capable of saying one thing only, and they say precious little of that these days. If you want to dress like a billboard or a bag lady, the British collections will not have disappointed you; if however you wanted to dress to

● Sarah Tisdall, dressed to shake governments. Photo courtesy of Camera Press

attract the opposite (or the same) sex rather than flyposters or philanthropists, you will have gone home empty-handed. To dress the body as something non-sexual is akin to putting a quilted cover on a toilet roll. *The only point in putting on clothes is to make someone else want to take them off.*

Anyone who possibly believes that they can serve some other purpose or make any other statement remains in a state of infantile paralysis – scared stiff of the real world, where problems cannot be solved by simply straightening one's tie or crumpling one's shirt.

THE FASHION P-R

"hard-nosed harpie" (sic)?

LYNNE FRANKS

 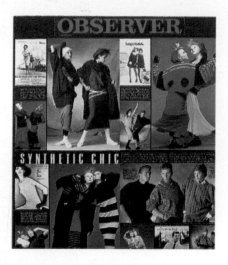 

In 1983, Brenda Polan interviewed me for a piece in THE GUARDIAN which acknowledged PRs as an 'army of hard-nosed, thick-skinned harpies, who deluge journalists with over-written press releases and gaudy invitations to champagne breakfasts!'

 Having asserted that this was not an adequate description of the PRs role, and having convinced Brenda that we were more than 'frock-pushers to fashion writers', I remember sticking my neck out, and saying that Britain was where all the new ideas, and all the excitement in fashion was coming from. International acknowledgement and recognition of that fact was what I, and other fashion PRs like myself, were striving towards at that time. We all knew that what was happening on the London catwalks was as innovative, as vital and as exciting as their established counterparts in Paris and Milan – our task, our whole raison d'etre if you like, two years ago, was to convince the world of that fact.

And now look what's happened – almost two years to the day after making that bold statement, we've achieved our goal. London is now very firmly on the map as a major source, a breeding-ground for creative thinking. In fashion terms, I think Liz Smith, fashion editor of *The London Standard*, summed it all up very simply. Just recently, after

another London Fashion Week had generated its justifiable excitement amongst the fashion press, she wrote that for British designers, practice had made perfect . . . 'Having won worldwide applause for their creative energy, and merely bemused tolerance for the amateurish way in which they (at first) channelled it, our designers have today won the respect of the world.' (Liz Smith)

Everything comes full-circle . . . cities have always vied with each other for superiority and prominence in terms of creativity, albeit in design or the Arts in general. For many years it was Paris, but other places have had their turn – Vienna, Berlin, Milan, New York – and now it's London. It may sound like another bold statement to make, but there are great innovators around today – the repercussions of what some of the creative talent is doing in London now will be just as permanent, just as far-reaching as what Cocteau and Diaghilev were doing earlier in the century. As an agency that is involved so closely with the styling and image of all our clients, be they fashion-related or otherwise, it's obviously essential that we keep in touch with what's going on in all aspects of the Arts and design. Our involvement with

fashion is really only one facet of a much greater awareness of creativity on all levels. I think that for us, it's a very exciting time to be in public relations.

The press aren't always kind though . . . our clients have to take their knocks from time to time too, but sometimes the controversy can generate more excitement, more retaliation than the praise. Clive James was a guest of honour at the collections over the recent London Fashion Week, and in his resulting piece for *The Observer*, he was characteristically less than kind! He described Wendy Dagworthy's brilliant winter collection as 'Yugoslavian army surplus', and condemned BodyMap's as a nightmare of 'shirred petroleum by-products, edged with flatworm ruffles'. Even Katharine Hamnett's sleeker, more tailored looks for the winter were dismissed in one quarter as 'London Transport bus conductress suits'. But I suppose it goes without saying that you can't please everyone, and this was an outsider's view. Perhaps a motor mechanic could review Clive James' next television offering!

One of the most important things to stress though, about PR, is that it is not merely press relations but public relations, and I think there's possibly a whole side to the

● A swirling riot of colour – Wendy Dagworthy's
Folklore Collection, Autumn/Winter '85 Chelsea Girl,
Autumn/Winter '83

business that is frequently overlooked, a side that people aren't aware of. Going back to the interview with Brenda a couple of years ago, I said very positively that it was important for people to understand that fashion was not a trivial nonsense involving an indulged minority. That the excitement generated by high fashion was what sells the rest of the clothing industry, which is, let's face it, a substantial British export, and the third largest employer in the country. To be able to promote this excitement and interest in a product is basically what our business is about, and we can channel the expertise that we've acquired in fashion into many other areas.

● Katharine Hamnett, Autumn/Winter '85

A professional attitude towards public relations is incredibly important, and a businesslike, orderly structure to the company. *i-D* magazine recently did a feature on the office which emphasised our unity as an agency – 'the Lynne Franks family!' We were flatteringly described as one of the most successful public realtions companies in the world – 'if not the most successful' (their words, not mine!), and though this was an obvious overstatement, our success is due to the professionalism that we've established over the years. At the time of writing, we have a total of twenty-six staff, including more than a dozen account executives with successful backgrounds

in design, journalism, retail buying, styling, marketing, advertising and of course, public relations. We work very closely with our clients on all aspects of consumer and

● Katharine Hamnett

corporate image projection, including exhibitions, fashion shows, photography, graphics, video production, advertising, fashion and style input, personality endorsements, and consumer promotional activity and sponsorship. Strategy is decided by the directors in consultation with key company personnel and then agreed with the client.

I think it would be fair to describe the office as a creative unit, which can put together in stages a highly personalised PR profile for an individual client. Analysing a client's particular needs, and then finding the appropriate market is the first step, before the cogs of the creative machine can be set in motion. Over the years our agency has built-up an extremely diverse range of non-fashion clients, such as

● Lynne Franks and Boy George at the Murjani Tent, London Fashion Week, March '85

Raleigh Bicycles, Lancaster Carpets, Carter-Wallace toiletries and most recently, Olympus Sports. It can be very rewarding to see the results of marrying these large companies

with the top creative people that we're involved with. Apart from the individual account executives that work directly with specific clients, we work closely with a number of talented individuals at the top of their professions – hair stylists, make-up artists, stylists like Caroline Baker, textile designers like The Cloth, and interior designer Ron Arad from One-Off.

To give an example, in 1983, TI Raleigh decided that they wanted to make cycling a more fashionable activity, and needed a new strategy to promote the Raleigh Collection, their new range of women's bikes. They employed this agency as an integral part of the project, and the result, for Raleigh, was an 80%

● Style Council wear Raleigh racing gear for video 'My Ever Changing Moods' February '84. Photos by: Peter Anderson, courtesy of Polydor Records

increase in sales. Raleigh is perhaps one of the best illustrations of where we've used our know-how in fashion and style to give a complete new identity to a well-established household name. Paul Weller of the Style Council rode a Raleigh in the video for 'My Ever Changing Moods', and Holly Johnson of Frankie Goes To Hollywood was photographed in *Vogue* wearing the Raleigh gear. All of a sudden cycling was a fashionable occupation, and Raleigh was the name to have on your back and under your bottom!

One thing that's been said of this agency is that we can always identify with the young, and I'd like very much to think that this is

Photo by: Mark Lebon

● The Lynne Franks family.

1. Jessica – daughter L.F. & Paul Howie
2. Lynne – L.F.
3. Joshua – son L.F. and P.H.
4. Daniella – L.F.
5. Stevie Stewart – Bodymap designer
6. Gabrielle – Katharine Hamnett sales
7. Lisa – Kath. Ham.
8. Eva Assayag – French P.R.
9. Evelyn – L.F.
10. Little Sara – L.F.
11. Marina "Booker-T." Jones
12. Debra "make the tea" Bourne – L.F.
13. Wendy Dagworthy – designer
14. Christine Bryan – L.F. associate director
15. Jennifer Corker – Jewellery designer
16. Bonnle – Bodymap
17. Sally-Ann – Bodymap
18. Heather Lambert, Agent at L.F.
19. Nancy – Katharine Hamnetts.
20. Lorna – Katharine Hamnetts.
21. Shinto – from Kath. Ham. Japan
22. Christine Woolnough – L.F.
23. Annette – L.F.
24. Mark – L.F.
25. Mohammed But – L.F. accountant.
26. Suzanne Flynn – L.F. nanny!
27. Liz Flynn – Wendy Dagworthy's P.A.

28. Paul Bernstock – designer
29. Marcus – L.F.
30. Thelma Spiers – Designer
31. David the driver – L.F.
32. Neale – L.F.
33. Vicky – L.F.
34. Sarah Beerbohm – L.F.
35. Marc – L.F.
36. Tracy – L.F.
37. Nicole – L.F.
38. Jennifer Bowman – L.F.
39. Paul Yacoumine – hairstylist
40. Hiotoshi – Jap. licensee Hamnett
41. Kim for L.F.
42. Chrissie Walsh – designer
43. Helen – The Cloth
44. Colin Harvey – designer, illustrator
45. Sue – L.F. P.A.
46. Motokazu, Jap licensee Hamnett
47. Paul Howie – L.F. managing director
48. Fraser – The Cloth
49. Alexander Currie – jewellery designer
50. Unknown
51. Unknown
52. Jon Prew – photographer
53. David – The Cloth
54. Ben Kelly
55. Charles

true. We enjoy working with creative young people like The Cloth and BodyMap, and I think it's the stimulus that comes from them that we can feed into marketing other products. We've done some very diverse things in the cause of 'marrying' some of our clients, but it's always worked – we've had BMX whizzkids doing their stuff on Lancaster Carpet to test the durability of the foam backing. We've had designers like Wendy Dagworthy and BodyMap working Courtelle to celebrate their 25th anniversary and lend weight to the term 'Technological Chic', and we've had The Cloth, Hilde Smith and Sue Clowes designing prints on Tricel to demonstrate its versa-

● Helen Manning, Fraser Taylor and Brian Bolger of The Cloth, designer prints for Tricel

tility as a high-fashion fibre.

The Courtelle Awards, which are now in their fifth year, have become a major event in the fashion calendar, and possibly the most significant development in our project to maintain the Courtelle name as a major force within the fashion industry. Courtelle's been in existence since 1959, and was immensely popular during the '60s and '70s, which I suppose you could call the heyday of the man-made fibre, but they needed a strong new identity to carry them confidently into the '80s – I think the Awards have successfully helped to achieve this. They offer both students and retailers the opportunity to gain

maximum exposure within the industry, and also to forge strong links between the technical and creative sides of fashion. The important people from the fashion industry are invited to attend the Awards show, and they really do remember the names behind the garments – the final winners have their designs made-up and retailed

● BodyMap at the Murjani Tent, Autumn/Winter '85

● BodyMap, Autumn/Winter '85

throughout the country, which gives them an enviable head start in launching their careers.

Last year, Courtelle celebrated their 25th Anniversary, and to mark the occasion they invited BodyMap, Wendy Dagworthy, Chrissie Walsh, Rachel Auburn and Helen Robinson of PX to design capsule collections in

Courtelle to reflect the excitement on the current British fashion scene. Sally Brampton did a marvellous piece in *The Observer* colour supplement which she called 'Synthetic Chic', incorporating photographs of the new designs by Tony McGee and Martin Brading, and black and white reproductions of early Courtelle ads from the '60s – John French photographs rubbing shoulders with BodyMap and PX! It was an incredibly strong visual spread which confirmed in the most powerful, immediate way, everything we'd already said about the durability of Courtelle, and its limitless potential.

Earlier, I emphasised my own very strong view that Britain is

● Reldan, Autumn '85 Collection

currently at the centre of creative fashion. Early in 1984, our office started working on press and public relations for the Harrogate Fashion Fair, an appointment which prompted mixed reactions from within the fashion press. I suppose this was because they could foresee a conflict with our involvement in London Fashion Week, but to my mind, Harrogate and London compliment each other perfectly, presenting us with the opportunity to work within all aspects of the British fashion industry. There are three distinct market areas in fashion – the designer merchandise shown during Fashion Week, which is sold to international buyers and

predominantly-London based stores; 'classic' medium to upper-priced fashion selling to department stores and boutiques throughout the world; and thirdly, what I

● Exterior of Murjani Designer Focus 'Tent', March '85

describe as the 'instant' young fashion market which sells nationally and internationally mid-season.

Harrogate is without doubt the most important venue in this country, outside of London, for British fashion. It remains constant on the fashion calendar, and provides a professional focal point for both buyers and exhibitors, with established names like Reldan, Alexon, Daks-Simpson and Aquascutum using Harrogate exclusively as their British showcase. There's a very special atmosphere at Harrogate which I don't think any other venue could provide – it compliments the collections perfectly.

Apart from Harrogate of course, our other major commitment to the fashion calendar is the Murjani Designer Focus, the central venue

● Barbara de Vries, Autumn/Winter '85 show at Olympia

in which London's major designer fashion shows are held during London Fashion Week. We've been working with Murjani on this for a number of years now,

and 'The Tent', as it's fondly become known, has achieved notoriety as London's first purpose-built venue for designer catwalk shows. We've seen some fantastic sights in the Tent over the past few seasons – for example, BodyMap's brilliant show last season which the press picked-up on as fashion's first-ever 'acid trip', an amazing spectacle which was as much a piece of theatre as a catwalk show – and Katharine Hamnet's 'Stay Alive' show, brilliantly staged, which had a marvellous ethnic feel to it, tribal drumming, a riot of swirling colours . . . incredibly exciting.

Creatively, I think the shows reached a peak in the Tent this season. Clive James may have dismissed Wendy's show as 'a lot of lighthearted skipping', with clothes 'moving too fast to be visible', but I think Geraldine Ranson was much nearer the mark, when she described the show in the *Sunday Telegraph* as a 'dizzy merry-go-round of dazzling colour!' Far more appropriate. The *Daily Mail* described Katharine as an 'armageddon' designer, which is quite heavy when you consider the implications of a tag like that, but then Katharine is deeply committed to her belief in world peace, and the armageddon connection doubtless came from the recent show – the oppressive 'Killing Fields' theme with the 'napalm' voice-over was chilling and deeply disturbing. It was intensely theatrical, but I can't personally think of a more powerful way for a designer to put her message across. The contrast between those rich, velvety looks, swathed in lace, and the despairing, apocalyptic world-view that Katharine chose for her backdrop was a compelling contradiction in terms.

Lynne Franks Public Relations has been in business now for fourteen years, but I feel that the time has never been so opportune for working with clients to forge fresh images. Both clients and consumer alike are now so aware of style and image . . . simple editorial coverage is no longer

sufficient. We have to follow through, starting with the basic product, and working with it relentlessly until we've created an image, established it as a brand

● Interior of Murjani Designer Focus 'Tent' in the grounds of the Commonwealth Institute, Kensington

leader, and if we possibly can, build a whole new cult around it. 1985 is only the beginning for a company like Lynne Franks Limited . . . we still have a great deal of work ahead in increasing the awareness of the consumer, the retailer and even the client of the limitless potential in the design, presentation and styling of a product's marketing, whether it be a dress, a bike or a shampoo.

Brenda Polan described me as the PR 'at whose name other PRs blanch and hardened hacks assume a hunted air' . . . that's a sobering thought. I'd hate to think that that's how everyone saw me! I just work hard at what I believe in, and I suppose I expect everybody else to do the same. I told *i-D* magazine that I expected 199% from my staff, and I do . . . if people find me daunting because of that

● Rich purples for Katharine Hamnett 'Think Global' show at Murjani Tent Autumn/Winter '85

then perhaps that's their problem, but I've always found that it gets results!'

INTERVIEWS WITH

JASPER CONRAN

AND

DIANA VREELAND

FIONA RUSSELL POWELL

The first time I met Jasper Conran was in fact fourteen hours before I was due to interview him at his Great Marlborough St. studio. My chance meeting with him was on the floor of the DJ booth at 'Taboo', fashion designer Leigh Bowery's weekly debauched soiree, where nearly every other young trendy fashion designer can be found, always completely drunk or in ecstasy.

So it was with some surprise that I should happen upon Jasper Conran, in Taboo of all places, who was drunk as a skunk (to coin a phrase).

At 4pm the following day, inside the spacious pine-wood floored studio, Jasper was nursing a very heavy hangover with great aplomb: 'I'm trying to pretend that it isn't there', and proved himself to be affable, rather sweet, anxious to consider every question carefully before committing himself to answering, charming to his assistants, fairly unaffected and – in general – exactly the opposite to what I had expected him to be, or rather, had been lead to expect by vicious tongues. The only question which was met with head-on refusal to comment on, was my request for more details on the Fashion Aid Show, which he waived to one side with a weary frown: 'so far, organising it has been a complete bloody nightmare and it might not even happen. It's such a long dreary story – I can't go into it.'

Now 25, he is smallish, dressed casually yet expensively and is one of those people who presses his fingertips together to form a church-spire whilst pausing thoughtfully and includes punctuation marks and full stops in his speech. We settled down in a small ante-room which serves as his office – white, sparse and clinically clean with a portrait of Coco Chanel on the wall, and got through two packets of Marlboro, a litre of apple juice and a tome's worth of salacious gossip which was for our delighted ears only . . .

FRP: Where do you live?
JC: I bought a house in Regent's Park about a year and a half ago. It's got a lovely garden.
FRP: Do you have any Habitat furniture in your home?
JC: Yes, a sofa.
FRP: Did you have to pay for it?
JC: Oh yes, I paid for it, I *certainly* paid for it.
FRP: How does it feel when you are referred to as a Superbrat?
JC: Er – I've been called it so often that it doesn't bother me anymore. You know, people call you so many things that if you let it affect you, then you're finished.
FRP: ARE you a Superbrat?
JC: I'm too old now but I think I probably was, yes . . . I think that's because – you know – in this life, if you want to get anything done, you can't be coy about it, you've got to do it. Of course, people aren't going to like it, but, so what? When I started, as a nineteen year old, people just did not set up their own companies and start working in their own companies, they always worked for other people.

FRP: Where did you get the money from to set up business?

JC: Well, it only costs £100 and I got it from my bank, from my bank overdraft in fact... Of course, maybe I wouldn't have got an overdraft if I hadn't had my name, but on the other hand, there's no way I'm going to feel ashamed about that.

FRP: In a way, it must be quite a burden having such famous parents, the way you have to work twice as hard to prove yourself in your own right... you must encounter a lot of jealousy and resentment?

JC: Yes, it's something that's always been levelled at me; 'ah yes, it must have been easy for him', but in fact, it's much worse, because, really, I didn't have the money and everybody thought I did have it. People like to say to themselves that it was all bought for me – which it never was. But at least I know that and it's enough for me to live with. If you have well-known parents then people always scrutinize what you do so much more and no matter what happens, you're always going to have that levelled at you and you just have to learn to live with it. But I reckon, other people have to live with other situations, so it's not the worse thing to happen for me. I just get on with my own life.

FRP: Do you ever wear other designer clothes?

JC: I used to, before I started doing men's clothes myself, but in fact, I take women's sizes because I'm too small to wear ordinary size men's clothes, so I just change the buttons on the same women's clothes.

FRP: Which designer clothes did you wear?

JC: Well, it depended on what I liked, but I used to wear Katharine Hamnett's clothes.

FRP: So you were never a label queen?

JC: Ha ha! Oh no, I'm not a label queen. When I'm working, I don't like to be uncomfortable, I just like wearing T-shirts and things.

FRP: Do you think people should wear different clothes for work/during the day and always dress up at night?

JC: I think the whole idea of clothes is, um... that's why I particularly admire someone like Katharine Hamnett who has really changed that image of 'dressing up'. You can wear BodyMap and Hamnett and feel fashionable and smart and comfortable and I like that whole atmosphere. It's not like it was five years ago which was high heels and short skirts – this whole Designer Dynasty thing, which I think is the most repulsive image because it has nothing to do with reality, the clothes on that programme are about power, it's all about rich women who do nothing, women who have all day to do nothing except their nails – there is so much more to life than spending time on your appearance. It's important of course but... with BodyMap and Hamnett and the navy blue Jean Muir dress, they've all got things in common, they've changed the expectations – women are expected by themselves, I think, it's what your own expectations of yourself are, your own inhibitions, nobody has actually said to you, 'I expect you to look like this' do you see what I mean, I'm not really putting it over right, am I?

FRP: I see what you're getting at, but I don't agree. I think there's a lot of pressure on women to 'look nice' and constantly renew their wardrobe. For instance, if a woman wears the same dress to many occasions, people tend to notice and criticise whereas a man can wear the same suit for ages and not get any comments –

JC: Do you really think so? Well, it depends on which social area you're talking about. If you're talking on a mass scale then, yes, sure that is an expectation, but so long as women allow that expectation to be fulfilled, as long as women are fed the line... it's mainly a commercial thing, the commercial idea that women are fed the line that they have to have healthy glossy hair and perfect skin, they are fed the line of this mythical so-called perfect woman, who of course, does not exist. In fashion photography – the women in those photos – it's a total set-up, it's trash, it doesn't exist. It's not movement, it's not the reality of wearing clothes at all.

FRP: Let's drop the question although I did have a Dynasty question for you, I was going to ask you what you thought of Joan Collin's wardrobe.

JC: I think it's horrible, it's absolutely hideous. I think Dynasty's a wonderful programme, I love it, it's almost like a drug. It's strange, it's television in its purest form. But the image Joan Collins, or rather Alexis, projects – her wardrobe is being fed to the masses. Every fifty year old woman now is being told that she ought to look like Joan Collins and why doesn't she, she says to herself when she looks in the mirror. But this is unreality, this woman in these outfits with fur-hoods, it's just gross.

FRP: But a lot of fifty year old women need and enjoy this fantasy.

JC: Yes, a fantasy, fine. But not to look like that, PLEASE!

FRP: Do you keep a diary?

JC: No – I don't like that kind of thing. What's past is past.

FRP: How do you reward yourself after a successful collection?

JC: I like to give parties. That's my best idea of a reward.

FRP: Getting pissed in other words!

JC: Yeah!

FRP: And what about after a bad collection?

JC: Well, you don't know when you're setting up the party if you're going to get a bad reception to the collection.

FRP: Have you had an unsuccessful collection?

JC: Yes. Quite often you're just left to realise that it wasn't good, people don't like telling me. I think, oh well, I've just got to do better. Of course, it hurts, but it's only your own fault if you've done the wrong thing.

FRP: Have you ever worn a skirt or a dress?

JC: Well – I've worn a kilt. Is that a skirt? Does that count? Actually, I loved wearing it, it was wonderful, because it has all these kick-pleats at the back, so it sort of swishes along.

FRP: Why were you wearing it? Was it for a Bobby Burns night?

JC: No, it was about three years ago. I just wore it because I liked the idea of wearing a kilt.

FRP: Have you read 'DV' – Diana Vreeland's autobiography?

JC: Yes, I love it. I think she's wonderful. Some people say that she's a liar, I say that anyone who can make up stories like that must be wonderful. If she really did do those things then she's fabulous. She's got style, which is a very inane thing to say about her, but that's the be-all-and-end-all of her really. She's got IT.

FRP: What's your favourite smell?

JC: I like the smell of lily-of-the-valley – the flower.

FRP: Where do you buy a) your groceries, b) your toiletries, c) your underwear?

JC: I buy my groceries at Camden Town market near where I live, it's a really nice street market and I buy my toiletries at Boots and I buy my underwear in Italy just because they have this particular brand that I like because they're cotton and comfortable. You know, men's underwear is not the easiest thing to wear. Marks and Spencer's underpants are so big. They're far too big for me. My Italian underwear is quite small.

FRP: Have you ever been anything other than a blond?

JC: Ah! Well, when it looked like I was going to go dark, I did something about it very quickly and I've never been anything else.

FRP: Some people say your designs are 'timeless' and others say that you're just 'standing still'. What do you say to both of those comments?

JC: I don't think that I am standing still-now.

FRP: So you agree that for a time you were, well, not being very adventurous?

JC: I think I probably was 'standing still' for a couple of years. But it's easy for people to criticise you, what they don't realise is that when your whole life is at stake, your home, all the money you've made, everything, depends on your work and selling it. I back the company, *my* company, and for a while it's inhibiting, you get frightened. But after a while, I decided I might as well stop pussyfooting around and over the last two seasons, I've put much more of me, my character into the clothes. Because you build it up and then you think, 'what am I doing this for if I'm not going to enjoy it?', which is what I was beginning not to. You know, you get pushed into a market, it sort of happens through the kind of people that buy your clothes and then you get inhibited, but then I thought, 'no, forget it, I don't want to be a has-been at twenty-four' and I changed my attitude. So I don't think I'm standing still. Timeless-yes I think I do make clothes that you can wear for a long time.

FRP: What do you think of your contempories?

JC: Which ones? I like people for different reasons. I think Crolla are relevant but I don't like the clothes really. I think BodyMap, Hamnett and Jean Muir are wonderful. Anybody that's good I like. They're all filling different markets. I think on the whole people are too narrow-minded.

FRP: What do you think is the best thing you've designed in your career so far?

JC: Oh God, I don't really work like that. Once I've done it, I don't think about it anymore, I go onto something else. Once I've designed a dress, I never look at it again.

FRP: Can you justify the price tags your clothes carry?

JC: Yes I can. The cloth is expensive and the make is expensive and I think my price tags are as relevant as anybody else's, in fact, they're cheaper than a lot of people's.

FRP: Tell me a little about these famous customers of yours. You do dress Princess Diana, don't you?

JC: Yes I do, there's no reason why I shouldn't.

FRP: Does she come here or do you go to the palace?

JC: It depends. I do have to go to the palace sometimes.

FRP: Because you design outfits exclusive to her, do you have to be tailor as well as designer and go armed with a tape-measure?

JC: Yes, but I'm not telling you her measurements! You know, I don't think of personalities, of people, when I'm designing an outfit. I treat them as an object, I don't care who wears them or buys them. There's so much made of who wears what, I think it's completely irrelevant. I don't believe in complete designer wardrobe dressing either, you can't buy an image, which is why I don't try to put over an image. People shouldn't buy clothes like that, it should be about their own personality. A lot of women are absolutely terrified of making their own decisions dress-wise, they like to be dictated to by the fashion magazines.

FRP: Jean-Paul Gaultier recently said: 'There are some people with no taste, but they are secure when they wear what is recognised as a coat of good taste'. I feel that that statement could apply particularly to some of your customers, ie: little taste, much money, no imagination. Is this presumptuous of me?

JC: Er, you see, the clothes themselves are expensive because of what goes into them, right? Um, I don't really know what to say to that . . . but I don't think I'm dictatorial in my attitude.

FRP: The people who buy your clothes can't really be bracketed within an age group, unlike, for instance, BodyMap wearers, who tend to be quite young.

JC: Yes, it's strange. My customers range from twenty to eighty. I think it's because I don't go out for this heavy identity thing – people don't wear a jacket of mine that says 'this is a twenty year old's jacket'. Although an eighty year old woman may look great in a BodyMap jacket or knit or whatever, she wouldn't feel comfortable, whereas if she wore one of my jackets, she wouldn't feel threatened by it.

FRP: Do you think you'll ever reach a point when you think you can't bear to look at another dress again?

JC: Yes, it happens quite frequently actually! But I like what I do, I like my job.

FRP: What do you think has been the most hideous/unflattering fashion trend over the last five years?

JC: That's difficult. I would say that I hate those 3" 'classic' court shoes. Those dreary high heels, stockings, short skirt, little cropped bolero jacket. It's

that Dynasty look again. I hate it, it looks so wrong. I can't bear what those 3″ heels do to the rest of the outfit.

FRP: Are you a good host?

JC: I try.

FRP: What does the word 'chic' mean to you?

JC: It means Joan Collins in Dynasty. The word itself is a vile, horrible word. It's like the word 'fashion', it doesn't encompass anything, it's a silly word. The word 'chic' has been used so loosely it's become completely bastardised, it means nothing.

FRP: I think the word 'chic' is supposed to give the impression that something is 'classy' and 'sophisticated' but it's been misused so much that it's actually got quite vulgar and common connotations.

JC: Absolutely. Well, it's a French word isn't it, which implies immaculate taste.'

FRP: What do you think of the Parisiens?

JC: I think they're full of shit. It's been said before but I feel that so much has come from England and all those fucking French houses are run on St. Martin's students. When people say 'Oh G____'s soooo fabulous' just don't give me that shit, I suppose Paris is a pretty city but it's full of shit – their one saving grace is that at least they recognised what was going on in England which no one here managed to do, but the French walked down the Kings Road or went to St. Martin's and then capitalised on what they saw. It makes me so cross. They're real pigs. So that's what I think of Paris. The way to deal with Parisiens is to treat them like shit before they treat you like shit.

FRP: How much are you worth?

JC: My turnover is now 1½ million a year from a £3000 overdraft.

DIANA VREELAND lives within her world whilst inside our world. She has the world in the palm of her hand. Imagine a small bubble inside a large bubble – hers is the large bubble and is impossible to burst. Inpenetrable yet all-seeing, she has unique but selective vision which has remained with her since the year dot. (Her age is indeterminable, since she has determined that this be so). To call her enigmatic would be pandering to her own publicity – she has made sure that she IS the enigma. Like a human-sense machine, she is able to seize upon such intangibles as a smell, a FEELING, an attitude, an atmosphere and turn the IDEA of something into a concrete form in one of her art/fashion exhibitions at the New York Metropolitan Museum.

This year, a book D.V. by Diana Vreeland appeared, telling more or less, the life and history of one Diana Vreeland. To all intents and purposes, it would seem to be an autobiography, however, Mrs Vreeland denies all knowledge of this book or the existence of any autobiography. Let us say then, that in her MEMOIRS, Mme Vreeland recalls with amazing clarity meetings with Diaghilev, Nijinsky and Buffalo Bill to being presented to King George and Queen Mary and a bloody drinking session in a speakeasy with Legs Diamond and Baby Face Nelson. She also explains her passion for the colour red and the French, no, Diana Vreeland NEVER EXPLAINS – she states. Although some have called her a 'menteuse', she certainly makes the ideal dinner party guest, with a story to

suit every occasion. She is the originator of such remarks as: 'The Civil War was nothing compared to the smell of a San Diego orange' and 'peanut butter is the greatest invention since Christianity'. Also heard to say 'A sense of humour always goes with elegance of mind', a philosophy which no doubt prompted her previous comments. When talking about her years as fashion editor at HARPER'S BAZAAR and editor-in-chief at VOGUE, she states: 'Editing is not just in magazines. I consider that editing should be in everything – thoughts, friendships, life'.

It is impossible to sum up the character of a woman such as Diana Vreeland, she has made sure of this, although the word 'impossible' probably does not exist in her vocabulary. It must be pointed out, that to this day, no journalist has ever got a satisfactory interview from Mrs Vreeland, so I suppose it was rather irreverent of me not to meet this challenge by being in her beloved city of Paris when the telephone interview took place. Thus, some of my questions which had to be posed by a third party, may have elicited a rather different response. Here then, is a five minute glimpse into the busy life of a woman who has dined and danced with kings, queens, gangsters, artists and prostitutes.

FRP: How do you choose your things for exhibitions in the Metropolitan Museum of Art?

DV: By going to places where I can get whatever it is we need. At the present moment we're doing an Indian show and we're getting things from London, from India and from all over Europe and all over America from private people and of course in India that's a different story.

FRP: Do you think that good taste is inherent or can it be bought?

DV: I believe that good taste, if you totally and completely apply yourself you can learn anything and once it gets into your bloodstream it's yours.

FRP: What do you think is the most hideous fashion trend in the last twenty years?

DV: I don't go in for hideous fashion trends and anyone who does is a fool.

FRP: Who do you think is the most overrated fashion designer today?

DV: I don't go in for overrated anything.

FRP: Did you take any notice of punk?

DV: Yes, and I enjoyed it . . . but I thought it was a waste of time – better things to do with your day.

FRP: You've been called the 'queen of fashion' – how does it feel to be so revered?

DV: Well, I've been called it, but only as a joke among my friends.

FRP: What is your fascination with clothes?

DV: That's an impossible thing to define. Why do you love your dog? Can you define it? Of course not!

FRP: Have you always been able to wear what you want or do you live up to an image?

DV: I have no image.

FRP: Do you think that age is any governor of style?

DV: I think experience is.

FRP: What do you think of Joan Collins' wardrobe?

DV: Who is Joan Collins?

FRP: She is the star of Dynasty, you know the TV soap opera.

DV: I don't go in for soaps.

FRP: What do you think of Nancy Reagan's wardrobe?

DV: I think she has an excellent wardrobe, has excellent taste and is very well turned out.

FRP: Are you a good hostess?

DV: No!

FRP: Everybody has a favourite Diana Vreeland story, which one is yours?

DV: I don't know any of them, you make your choice.

FRP: Which part of your career do you think has been the most satisfying?

DV: Well I've done three things; Vogue, Harpers Bazaar and the Metropolitan Museum. They've all been so satisfying because they came at different times, different periods in your life. They were all great.

FRP: Have you ever been in love with a dress?

DV: No.

FRP: What is the most vital item in your wardrobe?

DV: My shoes.

FRP: Where do you buy them?

DV: I buy all my clothes in Europe, either in Rome or in Paris. We have no shoemakers here you see.

FRP: What do you think of the Parisiens?

DV: Who, the Corsicans?

FRP: No, the Parisiens, people who live in Paris.

DV: Oh, the 'Parisiennes'. They're great people. Well I lived there for a long time. They're great.

FRP: What about their style, their dress?

DV: They've got great style, they are just wonderful people.

FRP: Where do you buy your groceries/toiletries/underwear?

DV: Where everybody else buys those things.

FRP: Who are your closest friends?

DV: I don't mention names in interviews.

FRP: What prompted you to write your autobiography?

DV: I haven't written my autobiography.

FRP: Who has?

DV: I don't know, I didn't even know it existed.

FRP: When was the last time you cried?

DV: Now that's an impossible question. Why in the world would I tell that to anyone and what makes you think I was crying lately? I'm asking you this. How did you ever think of such an outrageous question? No one should be proud of that question because that's not a nice question to ask anyone.

FRP: Do you think there will ever be a time when you are not involved in fashion?

DV: I shouldn't think so.

FRP: What's your favourite piece of furniture?

DV: Well I have very little furniture – so I have a bed. I guess my bed is my favourite.

FRP: What about other possessions – do you have a favourite?

DV: I don't have favourites. I've worked all my life, I don't worry about those sort of things, or think about them even.

FRP: Who does your hair?

DV: Dennis.

FRP: Tell me, what are you wearing at the moment?

DV: A dressing-gown, I'm dressing for dinner.

FRP: Well, Mrs Vreeland, thank you for giving me some of your time . . .

DV: That's all right, but I've never heard of such questions. Awfully gloomy, awfully gloomy . . . 'what do you hate the most', 'What's the worst thing you have ever heard of'. Don't you ever think up over there. I was born British, I know what is to be English and we were never that pessimistic.

FRP: What would you prefer to talk about?

DV: Oh, I like to be on the up side . . . Righto, good luck.

'.....SO GOOD THEY NAMED IT TWICE'

A second bite at the Big Apple

JOHN BADUM & KURT KILGUS

If Paris is the couture capital of the fashion world and London is the home of individualism, then New York is definitely the headquarters of BIG BUSINESS fashion. While the French capital brings to mind images of dedicated artisans toiling in ateliers, America's fashion capital conjures up scenes of boardroom bargaining and cold cash conglomerates.

The US is the land of free enterprise where a tie designer from Brooklyn, with some luck and lots of determination, can wind up heading a huge company designing everything from socks to suits, bed sheets to chocolates. But the blessings of success are mixed. Commercial success demands high sacrifices. Making a lot of money means selling to lots of people, and here, the great American demographics come to play. What's the market share? What was the overnight rating? Will it play in Peoria?

In the quest to get ahead, and in order to reach the most people there comes a point when fashion definitely becomes big business. Talented designers arrive on the scene and two years later, bowing to the pressures and demands of business, which calls for constant expansion, lose something of the qualities that made them special. Not to say that the product is bad. The work of American sportswear designers: Perry Ellis, Ralph Lauren, Calvin Klein, are known the world over. Go to Japan, a fashion capital known for inno-

vation and imagination and you'll see crowds of people wearing the familiar NY labels. But the business of fashion sometimes kills the personality of fashion. And after the burial, what's left?

What's left? New York's small scale designers. Men and women struggling to put forward their personal fashion vision. Young and not so young, serious but not straight, slightly to the left of center. They're determined to make their way. Here's a sampling:

DIANE PERNET

Diane Pernet has been in New York for eight years, living and working in a small space in Greenwich Village, far from the grinding Seventh Avenue machine. She's come to fashion after careers in film and photography and after a particularly unprofitable antique clothing venture. Pernet's love of antique clothing comes through in her romantic, nostalgic designs. She also has a keen sense of theatre and drama which carries through to presentation. Her opulently simple designs (contradictory adjectives that only make sense when you've seen Pernet's work) have been presented in such unusual venues as 'The House of Free Russia' and the Limelight Club,

when it was still a broken down church, tabu locations that Seventh Avenue officials would never consider. It's from these forums that Pernet presents her vision, her glorification of the woman's body. 'The clothes are made to enhance the woman' Pernet explains. 'Sensuality is the major thing. The way the fabric hits the body. Not your playboy bunny sexy, it's sensual.' But in spite of a devoted 'downtown' following and favorable press, the going is rough. Pernet's attention to detail, lush fabrics and small production add up to expensive clothes. Dollars for her orders are seen in direct competition with Bill Blass among others. 'The problem for me is the price point,' Pernet explains, 'When you are doing really expensive clothes you have a very small focused market and the market at that price point is buying labels basically. So until your name is a household word, that market is very, very small.'

It is hard to jump onto the Seventh Avenue merry-go-round but interest from abroad is giving a helping hand. The Japanese are particularly supportive of Pernet, as well as other small scale, 'sophisticated' designers. In fact Pernet has just signed a world

● Todd Oldham

● Abel Villarreal. Photo by: Albert Sanchez.

designer who shows in New York, also believes there is a new couture customer out there and he is counting on them for support. But a dramatic plunging neckline or a sensuously draped skirt do not necessarily carry great commercial potential in a country of t-shirts and blue jeans. And as with Pernet, price is also a problem. An outfit by Villarreal could cost well over $1.000. But Villarreal looks to the enigma of the corporate world with benign amusement and hopes for his backer in shining armour. And in the mean time, the twenty three year old designer, has covered ground in the fashion world that has commanded a growing respect from his peers. The press and

● Abel Villarreal

wide licensing agreement with Japan's Café Société. But the financial benefits of this will not be felt for a number of years and, in the mean time, Pernet remains in New York dealing with the problems of small scale design. Remembering the designer Charles James and his ruinous business career in this country, Pernet muses, 'We all know that creative design and individuality in America is the highway to bankruptcy and, of course, that is true. But I go on because I believe in what I do and I believe there is a market. I haven't touched my capacity yet.'

ABEL VILLARREAL

Abel Villarreal, a California-based

● Abel Villarreal. Photo by: Albert Sanchez.

● Abel Villarreal. Photo by: Albert Sanchez.

buyers are allies too, to a certain point. 'It's tricky,' Villarreal explains, 'There are those darting eyes out there, constantly looking for the newest and the latest. They are very helpful and supportive but they have the tendency to dart on to the next newest one. If you're able to use that as a stepping stone and get past it, that's great. It's what I'm trying to do.'

NORBURY AND OSUNA

While business deals are being signed and backers sought, David Norbury and Miguel Osuna have cleverly fashioned their own financial base. Two or three days a month of lucrative styling for television commercials allows this

design team the freedom to blaze their own financial trail, with only passing reverence to the usual procedures of Seventh Avenue. They may show out of their Second Avenue loft but their customers are some of the most trendiest shops in the US. As the business continues to grow, the team is mindful of the pitfalls that lay ahead. 'It reaches a stage,' Norbury says, 'when you wonder what you want out of the business. How much you want to sell out. (What you want out of your life.) They are dresses after all and it's your life.' But the team is determined to do it their way. 'I don't want to be a huge giant,' Norbury continues, 'but there's a lot of room to grow.' Norbury and

● Norbury and Osuna

Osuna, like the other designers, acknowledge that, at their level of business, their work is fair game for 'knocking off'. 'But,' Norbury states with a hyperbolic non-chalance, 'it phases me in no way, because we're always on to some-thing else.' Last year they designed a special line for the Japanese market under the auspices of Seibu department stores and this year they are working on experimental knitwear designs with French mills in Brittany.

TODD OLDHAM

While Pernet, Villarreal and Norbury and Osuna are struggling with the higher priced designer market, searching for that some-

● Todd Oldham

● Todd Oldham

times illusive new couture customer, designers like Todd Oldham and Marc Jacobs are offering more affordable clothes. But they still play the fashion game outside of the normal rules and their advanced, quirky styling has sometimes limited their com-mercial acceptance. Oldham, a Dallas based designer who only last year opened a full time 'CONGOVID' office in the New York garment center, brings humor in abundance to both his showroom and designs. The arriving buyer or editor is greeted (this season) by a gilt framed Mona Lisa coyly mounted askew on snagged taffetta. His miniature gold columns and hardened draped

fiberglass mix harmoniously with his shiny satin shirtings and too-high, too-wide jersey bell-bottoms. Oldham has commissioned prints from Ellen Birkenblit, a New York artist, who had never before seriously worked on textile designs.

Being in the vanguard of style while supporting a solvent business does at times become a squeeze that can pinch. But it is misinter-pretation by the press that can hurt the most. Although Europe affects fashion everywhere, Oldham feels the press sometimes misunder-stands and therefore mislabels young innovators in fashion, con-sidering them fashion duplicators rather than truly inspired. The designer states, 'It's hard for the

● Todd Oldham

press to understand that sometimes there is a universal consciousness or similar sensibilities in the fashion world.'

Undaunted, Oldham continues designing, pressing humour into garments once 'too-safe' to wear, bending the rules along the way and feeling what can fit into the market place, be saleable and still new. It is this irreverence to the rules that has put Oldham and fellow contemporary designer Marc Jacobs in a category ahead of most others in their field. A field, now, where others can only follow.

MARC JACOBS

Marc Jacobs is the latest to arrive on the scene. Fresh from Parsons

● Marc Jacobs

with an armful of student awards, he walked right in to a Seventh Avenue designing job, and, even if his humorous designs go above the head of many buyers, he has amazing autonomy in his new position and his work *is* selling. His no nonsense appraisal of the American fashion scene and his sense of humour and fun may provide the key to surviving and thriving in the American market. 'America is the home of sports-wear,' Jacobs says, 'and no one does it better, but I wouldn't call it fashion. I'd call it clothing. For instance, an Oxford shirt from Brooks Brothers is not fashion, it's clothing and there's a big differ-ence. Fashion is entertainment!'

● Marc Jacobs

And holding one or two trump cards from his retailing experience at Charivari, Jacobs approaches the challenges of big business as a game for his enjoyment. 'My fantasy, my trip,' he explains, 'is to see people wearing my clothes. You can say that means I want to make money but I really don't look at it that way. If I have enough money to survive, that's fine. I want to see people wearing my clothes. That's what I'm in it for and that's all there is to it.' But to fulfill his dream requires a keen sense of just how far you can go with the American public. 'I'm not into shocking people or intimidating them,' he explains. 'To me the best way to solve a problem is to follow the rules and bend them a little bit. How much you can get away with while still being accepted is a much harder thing to do than to go all the way. We could all come up with a thousand things that would freak people out, but why?'

The U.S.A. is definitely a mass market culture. And it often seems that quality, inventiveness and integrity take a back seat to sales in almost every area of our lives. But these and other fashion designers manage to co-exist with their omnipresent big brothers and so make a case for individualism in New York and in the U.S.

● Norbury and Osuna

THE EMPEROR'S NEW CLOTHES

日本ファッションのあゆみ

From Hanae Mori to post Holocaust

● CdG. Photo by: Paolo Roversi

Japanese fashion designers have played an active part in international stages today and Japan has become the centre of public interest in the fashion field. Although we suffered historically from the damage or shock caused by the Second World War, the fashion industry has been progressing steadily in Japan.

We would like to look at the fashion scene from the war and trace the bases of the movements happening today. We will divide it into three categories, such as; the gliding period, the taking-off period and the ascending period.

We can consider the period until the 1960's including pre- and post-war time as days for preparation. Fashion in Japan was getting into shape.

Until the '50s the Japanese fashion world was dominated by the teachers of dress-making schools and madams of coutures who stuck to the same old pre-war skills and methods. At the same time the main point of learning dress-making for young women was to be a good housewife, not as an occupation.

We can count that Dior's visit to Japan in 1953 was one of the events which stimulated a new movement in the fashion world. It is said that he was the first one

who showed beautiful forms of draping in Japan where only draughting was used. Almost the same time (1955), Hanae Mori who had already started to experiment with the draping method, showed her collection to the public – the very first one in Japan to open up the way to prêt-à-porter. In those days, of course, the word 'prêt-à-porter' had not been introduced yet and 'easy order' was the mainstream (*'easy order' is a Japanese-English expression and means high class order-made clothes for customers who have chosen the design from the samples.)

Fashion designers started to win recognition at last, when the Soen prize was founded by the Bunka Publishing Company (Bunka Shuppankyoku). This prize became the gateway for new and young talented designers.

1964, the year of the Tokyo Olympics was the peak of Japan economical growth. The fashion industry was not an exception. During this period they made contracts with many foreign fashion designers and brands. In

the domestic fashion scene, the designers such as Mitsuhiro Matsuda and Junko Koshina appeared and gained a following.

During the '70s 'Oil Shock' Japanese designers intended to find a market abroad. Those who were the pioneers of this movement were Kenzo, Issey Miyake and Kansai Yamamoto. In 1971 each one of them brought the new look, developed in Japan, into the first-class stages of fashion in Paris, New York and London. Kenzo especially showed his unique style – a combination of Western style draping and draughting or straight line idea, captured the reactionary mood. This seemed to be the time when his direction toward sans-couture sprouted. In response to this movement, such designers as Yohji Yamamoto and Rei Kawakubo began to seek possibilities abroad.

Also domestically it was the time when the small fashion manufacturers became powerful rapidly. Lots of boutiques opened in Aoyama and Harajuku, the fashionable area in Tokyo.

Apart from the clothes industry,

● Comme des Garçons January '85, courtesy of CdG. Photo by: Peter Lindbergh

第二次世界大戦という歴史的な衝撃を受けながらも、確実な進歩を続けてきた日本のファッション・シーンを、その戦後から助走期・離陸期・飛昇期と大きく3つに分類してふり返り、現在のムーブメントの基盤を探ってみたい。

第二次大戦をはさんだ1960年代までの時期は、日本におけるファッションがファッションらしい様相を形成するまでの準備(助走)期間とみてよいだろう。

それまで洋裁学校の教師や、戦前からの技術を伝承する洋装店のマダムが中心となっていた服飾界は、職業としてではなく、花嫁道具のひとつとして縫製技術を習得することが主であった。

それが新しい動きをみせるには、1953年のディオールの来日もひとつのきっかけとなっている。

それまで平面的な裁断方法をとっていたわが国に、女性のボディスをなぞった美しいフォルムの立体裁断をもっての彼の来日は、かなり大きなショックと驚きをもたらしたと聞く。まさに服は立体であるという実物が目の前につきつけられたのである。

同時期(1955年)、既に立体への試みをはじめていた森英恵は日本における第一回のコレクションを発表し、プレタポルテ(高級既成服)の道を開拓している。

もちろん、この頃プレタポルテということばは入ってきていず、イージーオーダー(高級注文服)が中心であった。

一方、文化出版局主催の装苑賞が創設され、新人の発掘が行なわれるようになる。やっとデザイナーの存在がクローズ・アップされてくるわけだ。

1964年の東京オリンピックを頂点に、日本は高度成長の時を迎える。

ファッション産業も例外ではなく、海外デザイナー、海外ブランドとの契約も著しい。

また、松田光弘、コシノ・ジュンコなどのスター性をプラスしたデザイナーたちが登場してくる。

そして、オイル・ショックに始まる70年代。日本のファッションはデザインの重要性を確認しつつ、海外進出を目ざしはじめる。その先導をつとめたのが、ケンゾー、三宅一生、山本寛斎である。

1971年、彼らはそれぞれ、パリ、ニューヨーク、ロンドンというファッションの檜舞台に、日本で育った新しい息吹を運びこんだのである。

特にケンゾーは、立体裁断を旨とする西欧技法に、逆に平面あるいは直線的なアイディアをプラスし、

大きな反響をよぶ。1973年からの、サンクチュールへの流れがこの時芽ぶいたといってもよいだろう。

こうした動きに呼応するかのように山本躍司、川久保玲といった面々がその可能性を海外に求めはじめる。

青山や原宿にブティックが乱立し、マンション・メーカーといわれる小規模のファッション企業が急速に台頭した時期でもある。

山口小夜子がパリ・プレタポルテに初めて登場し、東洋の神秘をアピールしたのもこの時期（1973年）だし、ニューヨークにおける須賀勇介（ヘア・デザイナー）の存在などファッション周辺の分野にも世界的なスターが登場している。

ファッションの多様化が著しくなるとともに各国の垣根が取りはらわれ、その交流がひんぱんになる。

日本のデザイナーたちも、森英恵の1977年のパリ・オートクチュールの参加をはじめ、ケンゾー、三宅一生、山本躍司、川久保玲などが世界のファッションの流れを左右するパワーをもち、インターナショナルに活躍している。

一方、企業サイドも、唯一オイル・ショックのダメージをものともせず、一千億企業が登場しはじめ、日本ばかりでなく、各国へその拠点を設けはじめている。

●杉山恒太郎
1948年東京生まれ。電通のCMプランナー。サントリーローヤル「ガウディ」のCMの企画をはじめ、本業にはしいなかたわら、詩人としての創作活動も行なう

先輩に触発され、刺激を受けた新人たちが毎日ファッション大賞新人賞などを足がかりに、第三世代ともいうべき新しい輪を形成、力強いステップを踏み出した。その代表選手が安部兼章、菱沼良樹、森孝行たちである。

社会・経済的にも日本のファッション・パワーが注目され、各新聞社がそのバック・アップやアピールに力をそそいでいる。毎日新聞のファッション大賞、新日新聞の世界のデザイナー招聘ショー、そして今年の4月に開催される読売新聞主催の東京コレクションがそうである。

政府もやっと腰をあげ、F・C・C（ファッション・コミュニティ・センター）の設立、W・F・F（ワールド・ファッション・フェアー）の開催など意欲的な動きが始まっている

質量ともに充実した日本のファッションが、パリ、ミラノ、ニューヨーク、ロンドンと同じ位置で活動し、影響しあい、今後80年代後半のファッション・シーンをリードしていくにちがいない。

田中宏　　　　　　　　　　　　　大塚陽子　　　　　　　　　　　　　大内順子

● Comme des Garçons, January '85, courtesy of CdG.
Photo by: Peter Lindbergh

this period around 1973 was very memorable in other fields of fashion as people became internationally known. For example, a Japanese fashion model, Sayoko Yamaguchi appeared on the catwalk in fashion shows in Paris; and also a hair designer, Yusuke Suga became popular in New York.

In accordance with the progress of the diversification of fashion, the barrier between countries disappeared and fashion exchange has come to be frequent.

Hanae Mori who took part in Paris haute couture, Kenzo, Issey Miyake, Yohji Yamamoto and Rei Kawakubo, have all become influential in the international fashion world. Not only the designers but also the fashion companies have grown, some have become multi-million companies in spite of the damage caused by the 'Oil Shock' and they've started to expand outside of Japan.

New talent inspired by those pioneers has emerged from the Mainichi Fashion New Talent Prize. This is the third generation. The representative designers among them are Kensho Abeno, Yoshiki Hishinuma and Takayuki Mori.

People have been paying attention to fashion in Japan in terms of social and economical influence and each of the major newspapers have been very supportive. Mainichi Fashion Prize was founded by Mainichi Newspaper, the International Designers Show sponsored by Asahi Newspaper and the Tokyo Collections, held this April were sponsored by Yomiuri Newspaper. Even the government has realised its importance and is working on organizing the F.C.C. (Fashion Community Centre) and sponsoring the W.F.F. (World Fashion Fair).

Japanese fashions have reached a high level in terms of both quality and quantity. The '80s will see Japanese fashion becoming very active and influential in Paris, Milan, New York and London, etc. and it will play a leading role in the fashion scene throughout the world.

DRESSING FOR ROYALTY

A wardrobe to please the nation

KRYSTINA KITSIS

Royal news is Big news. Princess Di' made it big at the beginning of the '80s in the midst of the Pop-Glam revival, sharing the limelight with Adam Ant, ABC and Boy George. She like them has become part of popular consciousness and like Wham! has been commodotised to the level of a household name.

But, unlike them her sovereignty puts her beyond the dictates of fashion: Diana won't be replaced the following year. Because she is the first royal in the last 150 years (with the exception of Wallis Simpson) to have a physical presence, she qualifies to be a media star. She is the cypher through which they royals can be made more accessible to the public eye. By imposing a stylish reality on an outdated tradition Diana makes royalty an attractive media package.

In a bizarre collage of sex gossip about a magistrate, reports of an armed siege and the announcement of Joan's departure from *Dynasty*, Princess Diana makes front page news because she too has breached convention by reversing the rules on dress. Her appearance at a public function wearing a damask silk dressing gown was her bravest gesture yet in demonstrating her mythical role as fashion leader. Fashion has always played on the myth of the separation between the boundaries of eroticism and modesty. Diana however,

never lets the mask of modesty slip, for fear of tainting the royal seal. Her steadfast femininity is fixed by a glaze of blondness and rose-pink pallor, reflective of the return to fixed sexual roles in an atmosphere of sexual repressiveness. She was at the forefront of the image of harmonious domesticity, making motherhood an attractive role. In this post-sixties liberated society the image of the family has become anathema to fashion and pregnancy a grossly unattractive state. But a fairytale romance transformed an ordinary jeans-clad girl into a taffeta gowned princess. She became our stylish madonna and instead of disappearing from the public domain, pregnancy became another image to humanise the royal face.

The demands for fiction in a time of austerity were met by this fairytale romance; Diana emerged like an oasis of salvation to lighten the load. She leads the matriarchal dominance of the contemporary royal line. The difference between tradition and fashion are marked in the difference between the Queen's newfound down-to-earth style and Diana's nouveau riche style of flaunting tradition. Time it seems has stopped for the Queen.

Her perennial parade through the spectrum of 'brights' then 'pastels' gives her an ageless quality. Homely florals and two-piece suits ensure the continuation of the Queen's dateless style. The ubiquitous square, box-shaped handbag which is either black or white and habitually looped over her arm seems to symbolise her sovereignty; it is the mark of timelessness. Fashion it seems is not for the Queen, Diana has taken over that vow. Youth permitted the Queen a brief period of flirtation with '50s figure moulding fashions but to overstep the limits goes against royal rules. Now she is stuck in a time warp where the demands of function and comfort leave little room for fashion and novelty.

Princess Diana seems to flaunt the image of tradition with her recent adoption of a more 'sexy' image. One of the greatest moments of irony occurred when Bruce Oldfield at his Gala party for Dr. Barnardo's cleverly reversed roles for Princess Diana and Joan Collins. The queen of *Dynasty* appeared virginally stylish and demure, whilst Diana scored a grand entrance in her Alexis Colby style shimmering gown with its plunging neckline and cut-away back.

● Mother and Baby. Photo by: Snowdon, courtesy of
Camera Press

She had done a double-take on the image of a larger-than-life princess in an imaginary world. By participating in the *Dynasty/Dallas* fantasy Diana has managed to fictionalise the image of sacred royalty.

Nevertheless, her daywear trends still bear the stamp of

● Princess Di backless with a lot of front. Photo courtesy of Syndication International

tradition and predictability. She epitomises the old in the new through the wearing of classical lines under the banner of designer labels. The individuality of each designer seems to be lost in their desire to follow the royal line. Fashion has ceased to be about

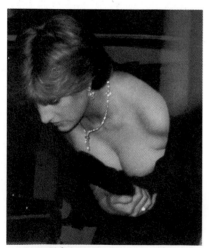
● Princess Di daring to go where no Royal has gone before. Photo courtesy of Rex Features

novelty; we no longer desire what is new but immerse ourselves in the process of renewal. Diana's lineage in tradition was established from the first moment of her first public engagement with Prince Charles when she appeared in her now famous black taffeta, low-cut gown. The Queen had worn an almost exact replica for her first formal picture after her accession in 1952, only the design wasn't by the Emanuels but Norman Hartnell. As fashion revolves around revivals Diana can be seen to be both adhering to tradition and leading fashion.

Unlike the Queen who was bred for her role, Diana as a mere mortal, has been forced to cultivate her role under the scrutiny of the public eye. By the singular act of a change of hairstyle she is launched into headline news; and by a similar thumbs down by the media, she is forced to alter it back to the way the public wants it. Her image is fashioned under the surveillance of the public eye. Her involvement with style is couched in the illusion of 'ordinariness' that she has now traded in for simulated glamour.

Princess Anne's recent appearance at the *British Academy Film and Television Awards* ceremony threatened to topple Diana from her number one spot. It was considered the most 'daring display by a royal yet'. She kept up the myth of her wayward character by arriving with a sensational addition of 'punk-pink' highlights in her hair. However, they did not quite qualify for the street, they were more in tune with Zandra's version of 'punk-chic'. But it kept her in line with the other loyal royals who remain faithful to the rules of co-ordinating accessories; Anne it seems has no time for fashions that breach the orthodox view of tradition, except when she's feeling a trifle daring. As in the intrepid '60s when she managed to raise her skirts and reveal a royal knee. Royalty in those days was forced to acknowledge fashion.

In the shadows of first his mother and now his wife stands Charles, a forlorn icon unable to carve himself an identifiable niche. Sober and puritan, he adheres to the tradition of uniform or suit. Flamboyance, a quality practised by their forebears is now, like fashion, equated with frivolity. Diana's stylish advice has only had

the effect of substituting tweeds for plainer clothes, but the same two buttons do up the same jacket cut. He only makes it into the media through a range of given stereotypes. His early 'dandy' and comic approach when he was a fan of the Goons gave him a more humane

● Punk Princess. Photo courtesy of Rex Features

and accessible image. But still no matter how many achievements he gains he never attains a star-studded role. Ideally Prince Charles and Bryan Ferry would like to swop roles. Ferry sees himself as an autonomous, titled and available Prince. Charles would love to be

● Andrew the Royal Robert Redford. Photo courtesy of Rex Features

Ferry's good-looking, playboy double.

Prince Andrew has youth and freedom on his side. Freed from the obligations to be King, power has become a great aphrodisiac to him. But he is forced to serve the duty-bound apprenticeship in the navy when really he would like to be a glam photographer like his uncle Tony and cousin Patrick. Still, at least he can be sexually transgressive through media hype. A ripple of muscle and pin-up on his arm gives him the desirable sex-symbol charm. Yet it is only

● Koo not so stark. Photo courtesy of Rex Features

through the association with glamorous women that the royal males score. In contrast to his brothers, Prince Edward takes a studious path, master-minding his way out of the public eye.

Margaret's decline from glamour-puss princess to royal

● Princess Margaret drink and cigarette optional accessories. Photo courtesy of Rex Features

renegade is once again symbolised by another anti-social act. By accepting the torch of wilful dissipation from her Uncle David, Margaret looks older and dejected, unlike her preserved contemporary Liz Taylor. Margaret used to outdo Liz in superstar status as leader of

● Mix 'n' Match Royal chic. Photo courtesy of Rex Features

● Elizabeth goes to Hollywood. Photo courtesy of Rex Features

the 'smartset'. She made smoking a stylised gesture by poising a holder at the tip of pursed lips. But the media have taken it upon themselves to chastise poor Margaret for committing, what is to them, an unforgivable sin. Stereotyped as the scapegoat, Margaret seems to have embraced middle-age: frumpy prints and out-of-step styles are all she can embrace.

Public scrutiny has not forced the ageing royals to use their wealth and influence to halt the ravages of age. The mark of the Queen's indifference to age seems to be contained in her image of spectacles worn with the splendour of full regalia. The sense of dignity royalty represents is completely negated by this addition of

● The new monarch – bejewelled and bespectacled. Photo courtesy of Rex Features

specs! Yet it is their very sense of ordinariness that the royals seem to want to convince us of. The return to a climate of restraint where the demands for stability seem more important than the breaking of boundaries means the royal family can be revived as a focal image as they bear the desired stamp of tradition. The British media always treat the royals with arch respect, highlighting a genuine royal dynasty that makes them the envy of the world. America's envy is expressed on the one hand, by modelling themselves on the royal dream in the form of Ronald and Nancy Reagan. And on the other, the *National Enquirer* sensationalises disrespect. It seems times change but values don't.

BIOGRAPHIES

JOHN BADUM is the director of sales and merchandising for L'Zinger, a trend setter in designer apparel manufacturing. He's well versed in every aspect of the business of fashion, having worked on Seventh Avenue since the early seventies, and he's also generally recognized as an important liaison to fashion's avant garde. He was an early and ardent supporter of some of the best of London's new designers including Leigh Bowery, Richard Torry, Gregory Davis and Judy Blame. And, as a freelance consultant, he advises some of the brightest new US design talent. He also has the largest museum quality collection of fun fur undergarments in New York.

JULIE BURCHILL writes for the Face and the Sunday Times. She once told Katharine Hammnet across a dinner table, "The reason why the young poor dress so much better than the young rich is that the young poor can't afford your clothes ... "

LYNNE FRANKS is the chairman of Lynne Franks Limited, one of the largest and most successful Public Relations companies in the UK. Originally a fashion consultant, Lynne Franks now handles a diverse range of clients, including Olympus Sports and Raleigh Bicycles. Fashion clients include Katharine Hamnett, BodyMap and Wendy Dagworthy. The company has been established for 14 years and the offices are situated in Covent Garden.
  Lynne Franks has two children, Joshua and Jessica, and lives in South London with her husband Paul Howie. She is a practising Buddhist.

LAURA HARDY studied at St. Martins where she gained a degree in Fashion Journalism. Whilst doing her degree she contributed to NEW MUSICAL EXPRESS and was Fashion Editor of short-lived teenage music mag, NEW SOUNDS NEW STYLES. From college she went to COMPANY Magazine as fashion assistant where she stayed for 2½ years. She has also been a regular contributor to the FACE and the OBSERVER, styled pop bands and worked on videos. She is now Fashion Editor of MIZZ (... it's fortnightly so she's not doing much on the side.)

DYLAN JONES trained as a graphic designer at Chelsea then St. Martin's School of Art, graduating in 1981. He then worked both as a photographer and model for Stephen Linard, Melissa Caplan, Takeo Kikuchi, HARPERS & QUEEN etc ... After a trip to Japan working for Men's Bigi he got involved with video production, whilst co-hosting The Gold Coast Club. The end of 1983 saw Dylan involved in i-D magazine ...

TERRY JONES (dog handler) art directed British Vogue between 1972-77, and has since worked as graphic consultant for other magazines including Donna, Italian Vogue, Pelle, German Vogue. Advertising includes work in Germany, Italy and the UK, from Phillip Morris Superlights to Fiorucci, Katharine Hamnett and Braun Shavers. Corporate i-D's include the classic PIL logo for Public Image and Murjani Designer Focus. Book compilations include THE MGM STORY, MASTERPIECES OF EROTIC PHOTOGRAPHY, the infamous NOT ANOTHER PUNK BOOK and PRIVATE VIEWING, published by New Leaf in 1983. Terry has also made videos – 'Rewind' for Catalyst, 'MAB Preview' for Chris Astridge and 'Electro Rex' for Wave. As well as editing i-D and working as Image Consultant for Fiorucci, he is learning Italian, how to cook and riding a bicycle.

KURT KILGUS gave up a promising career in brain surgery to become a freelance fashion art director. His advertisements for fashion designers and retailers have appeared in DETAILS, HARPER'S BAZAAR, VOGUE and W. He's continuing the writing he began while still an art director at Fairchild Publications (publishers of WOMEN'S WEAR DAILY) and is now a frequent contributor to VANITY FAIR. He's recently begun directing fashion videos for an independent production company. And all this is a result of an early career in brain surgery.

STEPHEN KING ex Hornsey, Walthamstow and Royal College of Art. He worked as an assistant to designer Tom Gilbey and as a shirt designer for Oliver Shirts of Wakefield. In 1972 he set up a design company – Otto Sports Limited, which although going well closed in 1979. Sat out the recession running a wholsesale company for a friend and private orders only. In 1981/2 he designed shirts and tops for major chain stores, (Top Man etc.), but went bankrupt. Opened the Stephen King shop in the Kings Road on February 14th 1983 and hasn't looked back since.

KRYSTINA KITSIS took a degree in Fashion and Textile design at St. Martin's School of Art. Then, a postgraduate master degree in cultural history where she wrote a thesis titled: 'Perspectives on Fashion: Wealth, Sexuality and Images.' Currently she is a freelance writer, assistant editor with ZG magazine, lectures in fashion and photography and is working on a book called FASHION AND FETISH.

PAUL MORLEY takes time. What he does with it is some people's guess. Known best as a journalist with the NME, a member of the Art of Noise, someone who had something to do with Frankie Goes to Hollywood and designer of Zang Tuum Tumb, his avowed mission is to discover truths and state them. His favourite comedians are Barry Humphries and Steve Martin, he enjoys drinking and forgetting and acknowledges the influence of Marc Bolan's 'Electric Warrior', Gertrude Stein's 'How to Write', page 203 of his copy of 'Finnegan's Wake' and Eugene Ionesco's 'Rhinoceros'. He is in love with one woman and the twentieth century. What's more, he forgets ...

THOM O'DWYER – 'like Scarlet O'Hara, Ava Gardner and Truman Capote' – was born and bred in the Deep South of the USA.

He studied fashion design and illustration at Parsons in New York. In 1970 he won a scholarship to London's St. Martin's School of Art, and has been in London ever since. He worked for a well-known London based fashion consultancy where he was Men's Fashion Director, and freelanced for a number of fashion, style and trade publications throughout the world. In 1981 he went to work for MEN'S WEAR, the UK men's fashion trade's bible, as Fashion Writer. He is still there – preaching the Word and hoping that a few are listening. Thom appears on television and radio, and is much sought after as a lecturer. He recently chaired the ICA's men's wear seminar during its successful Talking Clothes/Performing Clothes event. Well known for his wit, insight into the Wonderful World of Fashion, and unique style, he is also a self-confessed Fashion Victim. 'Fashion is a drug, and I am an addict', is Thom's favourite homily.

He adores Chinese food, BodyMap, holy water and Lynne Franks (in that order). He loathes a certain blonde-haired fashion editor, the 'In Crowd', good taste, and anything REMOTELY healthy (including free range eggs).

JUNKO OUCHI was born in Shanghai and graduated from Aoyama Gapuin University. She spends most of her time as a fashion journalist on radio and for leading Japanese newspapers and magazines. She has also written books and has been involved in costume and stage set design for the theatre. She is a committee member of the Tokyo Collections, the World Fashion Fair and the Fashion Community Centre.

FIONA RUSSELL POWELL has interviewed the famous for the FACE; INTERVIEW in New York; TIME OUT; GIL in Paris and other such stylishly revered journals. At fifteen she was expelled from public school. She is twenty-two years old.

MIKEL ROSEN, since leaving school, decided to work in fashion or textiles somehow. He graduated from St Martin's School of Art in 1976, to work with a multitude of fashion names. Internationally, in a promotional way, his work, under the banner of MIKEL ROSEN PRODUCTIONS, has handled major projects – for example 'TEXSTYLES' from the Crafts Council, 'FUSING FORCES' from the N.A.D.F.A.S. and 'PHYSICAL CHEMISTRY' from the United Nations and the G.L.C. for the International Year of the Youth 1985.

He is actively involved, twice a year, with LONDON FASHION WEEK with numerous designers presenting their collections – from Jean Muir to BodyMap or Jasper Conran to Wendy Dagworthy.

Other show consultancies involve companies such as Marks & Spencer, Richards, Next, Benneton, Courtaulds, Mondi, British Airways and Pretty Polly.

For five years, Mikel Rosen was a senior lecturer at Middlesex Polytechnic.

Before establishing his company, Mikel designed for Basile and Trell in Milan and Jeff Banks and Inega in London. He has appeared on Pebble Mill, 6.55 Special and South of Watford to discuss the work of Mikel Rosen Productions.

STEVIE STEWART is one half of the newsworthy, headline grabbing fashion design team BODYMAP. She studied at Middlesex Polytechnic between 1979-1982 and obtained a first class honours degree in fashion and textiles before forming the company with fellow student David Holah. BodyMap's designs have sold world-wide in such prestigious shops as Browns, Joseph, Searcy's, Bloomingdales and Harrods. They have appeared in EVERY fashion magazine and have been commented on by every fashion expert. Stevie relaxes amongst London's seedier celebrities and can be seen shaking her hips in many of the capital's 'one-night-stand' nightspots ...

VAUGHN TOULOUSE was born in St. Helier, Old Jersey, 25 years ago, and decided from an early age that his vocation would lie in entertainment. After telling a disbelieving careers adviser at school he was going to be a pop star, Vaughn set out to prove him wrong, eventually winding up as the singer/songwriter in the short-lived Department – S and scoring a 'one hit wonder' with 'Is Vic There?' in 1980.

Has worked part time writing for the FACE, (check issue No. 1) for his personal account of his teenage 'on the road with the Clash' tour guide.

Recently has turned his talents to club running and DJing at Do Do's, monthly in London, Birmingham and Liverpool, Saturday nights at the Wag and various one-offs, 'if it sounds like a good time' anywhere.

He has returned to recording 'music for pleasure', solo this time, 'I aim to fill that gap left by Tom Jones!'

'I've set out here to interview a cross section of club-goers, each choosing their personal places of party and about the gear they wear to party in, they speak for themselves, I've gone for the personal touch!'

TOM WATKINS trained as an interior designer, formed XL just three years ago with graphics specialist Royston Edwards. The company is now established as one of the leading graphics and marketing houses for the music business in the capital, having serviced almost every major record label and devised campaigns for artists including Frankie Goes To Hollywood, Wham!, Duran Duran, The Art of Noise and Kim Wilde. Having earned a reputation as innovative 'image makers', XL has since expanded to incorporate two sister companies – Big Features (commercials and promos) and Massive Mangagement, the pop band management umbrella which is now Tom's major concern.

IAIN R. WEBB has never considered himself to be 'fashionable', even so he is now Fashion Editor of BLITZ magazine. He studied at St. Martin's ('but then didn't everyone else?' – Ed); worked under Zandra Rhodes for OVER 21 (and numerous fashion journals); and sat behind Sally Brampton at the seasonal collections 'but then didn't everyone else?' – Ed). His first memory is of a pair of tartan Rupert Bear trews. He has since

THE FASHION YEAR

Complete your collection of the Fashion Year books. All the glamour, excitement and style of the international world of fashion during one of its most innovative periods.

VOLUME I

Includes exclusive interviews with the leading pioneers in the design world – Lagerfeld, Miyake, Armani and Alaia. Special features on Princess Diana, the Japanese influence, Hats and Swimwear.

VOLUME II

Focus on leather, the influence of music and film on dress, street fashion, surveys of the collections from New York, London, Paris, Milan and Japan. Also penetrating examinations of the fashion business, styling and fashion writing.

Both volumes include original and distinctive photographs and illustrations.

Available from bookshops or order direct from Zomba Books (price includes postage & packing but only available to addresses in the UK and Northern Ireland).

A discount of £1.00 per book will be allowed on orders for two books or more. Or why not order all three volumes and take advantage of the special price of £20.55.

---

orders to Zomba Books, 165-167 Willesden High Road, London NW10 2SG.

Fashion Year Vol I @ £8.20, Fashion Year Vol II @ £8.20, Fashion Year Vol III @ £9.15, Volumes I, II, III sets @ £20.55.

enclose a cheque/P.O. made payable to Zomba Books .